SILVER + STONE

SILVER + STONE

PROFILES
OF AMERICAN INDIAN
JEWELERS

MARK BAHTI

RIO NUEVO PUBLISHERS
TUCSON, ARIZONA

CONTENTS

Preface 7

Introduction 8

THE ARTISTS

Alex Beeshligaii 18

George and Donna Bennett and Family 22

Roland Brady 26

Joseph and Mary Calabaza and Family 30

Michael and Mark Roanhorse Crawford 34

Bernard Dawahoya 40

Dennis and Nancy Edaakie and Family 44

Cheyenne Harris 48

Ferdinand and Sylvia Hooee 52

Jackson Family 56

Carlton and Julie Jamon and Family 62

Al Joe 66

Frances and George Jones 70

Dorothy Poleyma and Raymond Kyasyousie 72

LaRance–Denipah Family 76

Allison Lee 82

Clarence and Russell Lee 88

Jake Livingston 92

Gerald Lomaventema 96

Mary C. Lovato and Family 100

Ray Lovato Sr. 106

Rick Manuel 110

Victor Lee Masayesva 112

Wayne Muskett 116

Farron Naka'waywisa 120

Albert Nells 122

Gibson Nez 126

Loren Panteah and Yolanda Laate 130

Allen Pooyouma 134

Angie Reano Owens and Family 138

Nick and Me-Wee Rosetta 142

Maria Samora 144

Cody A. Sanderson 148

Elmer Satala Jr. 152

Raynard Scott 154

Raymond Sequaptewa 158

Howard and Patricia Sice 162

Roger Skeet Jr. 166

Jason Takala Sr. 168

Jack and Mary Tom 172

Roger Tsabetsaye Sr. 176

Orville Tsinnie 178

Ed and Jennie Vicenti 184

Bryant Waatsa Sr. 190

Lorraine and Duwayne Waatsa 194

Lee Weebothee 196

Alton and Kee Yazzie 200

Steve Yellowhorse 204

Acknowledgments 208

Glossary 209

Indian Markets and Fairs 211

PREFACE

FIRST, A FEW WORDS about what makes this book about Native American jewelry different from all the rest. It is different in many ways, but primarily for one reason: I wanted to present the work of a wide cross-section of American Indian jewelry artists of the Southwest in the context of their lives. I wanted to present them—and their work—as I know them, as members of families, as parts of a community, as individuals, not neatly packaged stereotypes.

Great pains were taken to ensure not only accuracy, but also the correct tone, the correct voice: it is not just what you say, it is also how you say it. In each case the artists profiled received copies of my initial notes to review and correct. The process was repeated with a working draft and again with the final draft. Sometimes the exchange went on longer—whatever it took to make it right, as I was ever cognizant of the fact that these stories are *their* lives, and I am merely relating them to you (that said, I bear full responsibility for any errors that may have crept in). Every word had to have the artist's approval. I hope that respect is evident in the work.

If that sounds like a lot of work, well, it was. But don't be fooled—it was also a lot of fun. Friendships were rekindled, new friendships were begun, and all to the accompaniment of stories exchanged. These included funny stories accompanied by a smile or by peals and tears of laughter, and sad stories and tender stories, and stories accompanied by a long, thoughtful moment of silence.

OPPOSITE PAGE: *Necklace by Al Joe.*

INTRODUCTION

THE STORY OF SOUTHWEST INDIAN stone and shell jewelry is an ancient one. The story of how a Navajo ironworker named Atsidi Sani added silver to that tradition in the 1850s is oft repeated, as is how the Zuni and eventually the Hopi began to work silver by the turn of the twentieth century, trading among themselves—as well as supplying the tourists coming out on the Santa Fe Railroad and staying in the elegant new Harvey Houses that were built along the way.

What is usually lost in that historical narrative is the personal. The early silversmiths were players on a historical stage: besides Atsidi Sani (Old Smith), there were Atsidi Chon (Ugly Smith), who traded his silver for livestock at Zuni and later taught his host, La:niyahdi, who in turn traded at Hopi and taught his host, Sikyatala (Yellow Light). What this book does is provide the reader with a closer look at more recent actors on that stage.

In putting this book together, I've tried to choose artists who, for the most part, haven't been heard from directly before. I've included people from a wide range of tribes and age groups, people at different points in their careers, people employing different techniques and approaches in their work. And I've wanted to humanize the story of contemporary Native American jewelry, not documenting how many ribbons somebody has won at an Indian arts show, but finding out why these people make the effort to create this work. These are human stories, not romanticized stories; time and again, you'll meet someone who started making jewelry because he lost his job at the service station, or who got reeled back into it years after trying it and initially not liking it.

ABOVE: Reversible pendant by Lee Weebothee.

I have tried almost all the techniques used by the people in this book, and my attempts haven't always been successful. But knowing the tools and the pitfalls means I was speaking the same language as the artists during the interviews—even if we weren't both speaking English. If you've never worked silver or stone, there's a glossary at the end of this book that should introduce you to some terms you'll encounter.

A note about clans, which are frequently mentioned in the biographies of the Navajo silversmiths: in Navajo culture, you're born *to* your mother's clan, and born *for* your father's. Further, some Navajos are insistent about prefacing their self-introduction with their clans, while others are not inclined to offer that information.

Navajos and Pueblo Indians were working metals by the nineteenth century, using skills they'd learned from the Europeans who were swarming onto their land. At first, their metalworking was limited to iron bridle bits and ornaments for bridles, with occasional simple bracelets, rings, or earrings fashioned from scraps of copper or brass. It's possible that a few early smiths were scattered across Navajoland by the middle of the nineteenth century, but old stories credit one man as the first metalworker among the Navajos. In 1938, when there were still a few people living who remembered the infamous Long Walk back from their imprisonment at Fort Sumner, New Mexico, a young anthropologist named John Adair recorded the story of the first Navajo to learn silversmithing. About

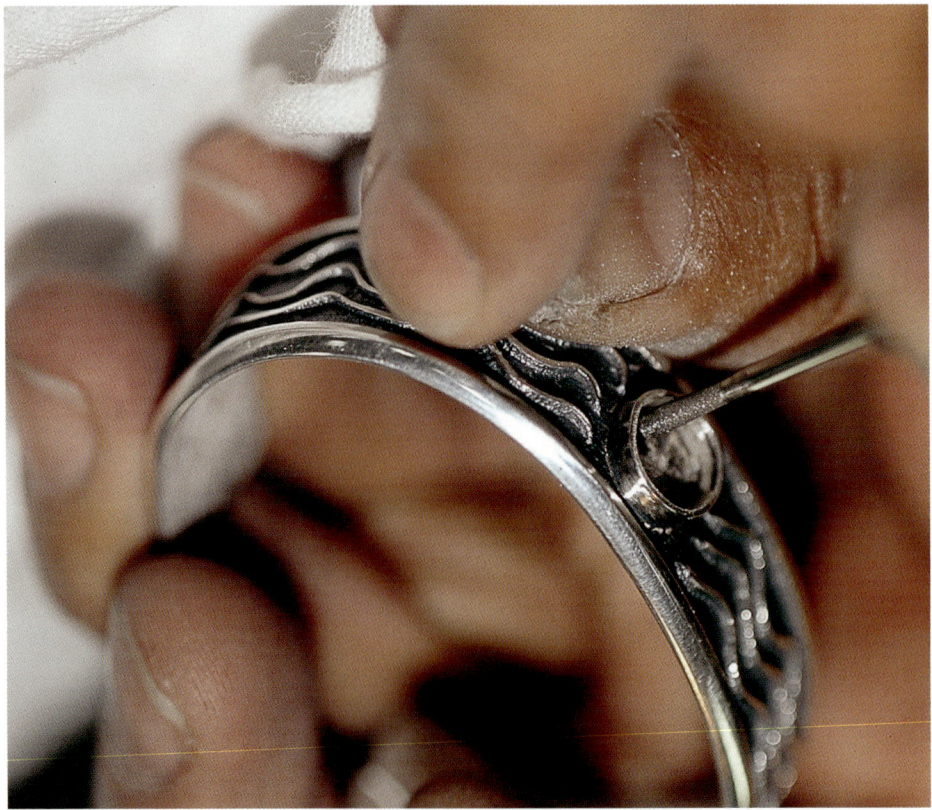

Steve LaRance.

1850, Atsidi Sani learned how to work iron from a smith the Navajos remember as Nakai Tsosi ("Thin Mexican"). This was about the time that the United States Army established Fort Defiance in the heart of Navajo country as part of its effort to gain control over Dinetah—Navajoland. One of the American civil agents who based himself in the Chuska Mountains north of Fort Defiance brought with him an American blacksmith named George Carter and a Mexican silversmith named Juan Anea, who had contact with many Navajos, apparently including Atsidi Sani. It seems likely that the 1860–1863 imprisonment of thousands of Navajos at Fort Sumner provided an opportunity for more Navajos to gain the new skill more quickly. Military reports from the time suggest that the Navajos were already making simple bracelets, rings, and earrings. Their skill is attested to by the fact that they were also forging some of the metal ration tickets issued. (Fair play, considering the fact that civilian contractors were short-rationing the Navajos with such poor-quality foodstuffs that even the military commander of Fort Sumner was outraged.)

Exactly when the Navajos began working silver is a matter of some dispute, but clearly silver (from Mexican and, later, American silver coins) became more widely available to them once they were settled back in their old territory in 1869, and the ensuing peace allowed once again for trade and travel.

Silverworking skills spread steadily, if somewhat slowly at first, with fathers teaching their sons and clan nephews, keeping this valuable new occupation within the extended kinship system. It also spread along established intertribal trading routes through trading relationships. By 1872, a Navajo silversmith named Atsidi Chon, who made annual extended visits to Zuni to trade silver for livestock and other goods, had taught his Zuni host, La:niyahdi. (We like to think that Indian silver was inexpensive in the old days, but according to Zunis interviewed by anthropologist John Adair, it was not. As an example, a concha belt brought a team of horses in trade.) The process repeated itself in another tribe when in 1898 La:niyahdi—who visited Hopiland to profit from his silverworking skills, just as Atsidi Chon had done among the Zunis—agreed to teach Sikyatala, his Hopi host. (It is worth noting that though from different Pueblo groups, they were related; both were members of the Mustard Clan.)

John Lorenzo Hubbell and C. N. Cotton operated the Ganado Trading Post in what is now Arizona, beginning about 1884. Good businessmen, they were quick to recognize the commercial potential of Navajo jewelry. In addition to paying Navajo silversmiths to teach other Navajos the craft, they brought in Mexican smiths to teach them as well—perhaps an indication that most Navajo silversmiths preferred to teach only family members. Hubbell, Cotton, and other traders, however, had their eyes on a potentially larger market: tourists, who would ultimately demand more work from more silversmiths. Indeed, some silversmiths found they could make a living working silver rather than depending upon livestock, farming, and hunting.

Much of the work was designed to fit the tourist notion of what Indian jewelry was "supposed" to look like. Ironic, considering they had never seen it before. Nonetheless, jewelry adorned with swastikas (from the Sanskrit words *su* and *vasti*, meaning "well-being"; also known as whirling log or fylfot), horses, tipis, arrows, thunderbirds, and the like flourished. Much of it was lightweight, the result of tourists' preference for lighter, more comfortable jewelry. This style, dubbed "Fred Harvey jewelry" after the major buyer, could more accurately be called "railroad jewelry," reflecting the origin of the market for these items. By the 1920s the number of traders had increased, and so had the competition. It was during the 1920s that manufactured copies of Indian jewelry began to appear. It seems to have started in the Southwest, with jewelry largely manufactured on hydraulic presses (often run by Indian craftspeople), but it was soon being produced outside the Southwest—from Denver to New York—and shipped in to be sold as Indian jewelry by a wide variety of outlets. (Eventually this led to the founding of the Indian Arts and Crafts Board to promote and protect handmade Indian art.)

Trading post owners, seeking a competitive edge over one another, sought to develop regional styles, as seen in the varieties of rugs woven by weavers with whom the traders did business. No longer was one post selling Navajo rugs in direct competition with another; instead, many sought to sell a pattern or style different from most of the others (hence, the rise of styles such as Two Grey Hills, Ganado Red, and Crystal). Similarly, traders at Zuni wanted to be able to market a jewelry style that was different from the jewelry that all other Indian tribes were producing. The Museum of Northern Arizona also helped develop and encouraged a distinctive jewelry style for the Hopis, so they would not be competing against Zuni or Navajo silversmiths from their remote mesa villages. Consequently, by the 1940s Zunis were focusing more on lapidary work (using shell and stone); plain silver jewelry and silver jewelry with a few turquoise settings were generally left to Navajo smiths, and the Hopis were beginning to focus on overlay work, using Hopi textile and pottery designs.

But from the beginning, most Indian silversmiths were adapting and adopting designs, materials, tools, and techniques to suit themselves. The market (both Indian and non-Indian) certainly has had a hand in shaping the product, but the market is fickle, and the artists are the ones who ultimately determine what will be made. Through the late 1960s and into the very early 1970s, people bemoaned the "fact" that "they aren't making them like they used to" and shied away from innovative work because it wasn't "traditional." Forget that squash-blossom necklaces were hardly traditional when *they* first appeared in the 1870s. People seemed to feel that Indian art and Indian culture were either disappearing or were supposed to be kept preserved under a bell jar, unchanging; they failed to recognize that change is a part of *all* living cultures.

OPPOSITE: *In the studio of Edward Charlie Shawes and Mark Roanhorse Crawford.*

By the 1970s the market had begun to shift and embrace innovative or "contemporary" work with a vengeance. The shift became so pronounced that today many innovative artists find, when they return to the annual shows where they sell their work, that buyers may be more interested in seeing what "new" work they have done than the style they were creating as recently as last year. Fortunately, the diversity of collectors and admirers of Indian jewelry today is such that almost any artist can find a market for his or her style of work.

☾

Is Native American jewelry a form of personal artistic expression? For some of the families you'll meet in this book, all the decisions about jewelry-making are very pragmatic; they make jewelry only in the gaps between other, more certain economic opportunities, or they work only on the sorts of pieces they know will sell well. Frances Jones (Navajo), for example, tends to be production-oriented. She sand-casts her pieces and prefers to sell them rough (unfinished) because she hates to buff and polish. She'd rather take less money for rough work than have to mess with what is arguably the dirtiest and most tedious part of the jewelry-making process.

Others are interested in making jewelry as a way of approaching a design problem, or working on some technical issue that may open up new possibilities. Then the question may become, "Now that I've done this, will anyone want to buy it?"

How do these artists get their start? There's no single career path. Since World War II, beginning with the GI Bill, it's been possible to take classes in jewelry-making and other traditional arts. Before that, and to this day, many silversmiths began as children watching their parents or grandparents do the work. Not helping, just watching. Silversmithing requires tremendous patience, and children generally must prove they have that patience, and a dedicated level of interest, by quietly observing long before they're allowed to pick up a tool. From there, it's a matter of mastering one skill at a time. Budding artisans may begin by doing mundane preliminary tasks, like sorting turquoise stones; some start out at the end of the process, doing the messy, dirty chore of buffing, and working their way back.

Then, of course, there are those who, to the everlasting frustration of the rest of us, simply have a gift for the work.

Just as each silversmith entered the field in a slightly different way, each has his or her own style. There's a multiplicity of approaches to this work, and generally one pair of earrings won't look much like one from the next artist. You can always see the individual artist in the good work. The cross is a Navajo symbol for stars, but it means something entirely different to Navajo artist Roland Brady, a devout Catholic, and you can see that in his jewelry. Albert Nells is a traditional Navajo who uses only the colors of the four directions and the stones associated with them, reflecting who he is.

Born and raised in the Southwest, I am the oldest son of a man who came West to study anthropology at the University of New Mexico, under the GI Bill. My dad soon found that the living cultures of American Indians held more interest and relevance for him than excavating their pasts. Until his death in 1972 he made a living in the Indian arts business and wrote three of the most enduring volumes on the arts and crafts, history, and religions of the tribes of the American Southwest, as well as assisting in the struggle for voting rights, mineral rights, water rights, land claims, and health, education, and economic development for the tribes. The relationships he established in that process nurture and sustain and inspire me to this day.

I grew up traveling with my dad to reservations across the Southwest, to Indian art exhibitions where he judged, staying in hogans and pueblos and Route 66 motels, and camping out. Going to Shalako at Zuni in winter, attending Katsina dances in the plazas and the kivas at Hopi, spending feast days at Rio Grande pueblos … listening to my father, watching and learning from my father. Many of the artists I work with today I have known since I was little; many more I have known since we *both* were little. When I started my family it was natural for me to take my daughter, Kim, and my son Yuri with me on my trips, as my father had done with me. Currently I still travel with my youngest son, Santiago, and of course, with Emmi, my other half. Perhaps in a few years I will travel with my grandchildren, and they will have a chance to meet and play with the grandchildren and great-grandchildren of artist-friends across the Southwest. And that is the whole point: from my perspective and, I believe, from that of most of the folks with whom I work, this business, the Indian arts business, is not about business so much as it is about relationships, and that is what I hope is conveyed by the words of the artists profiled in this volume.

And this I learned, by word and example, from my late father, to whom this volume is gratefully dedicated.

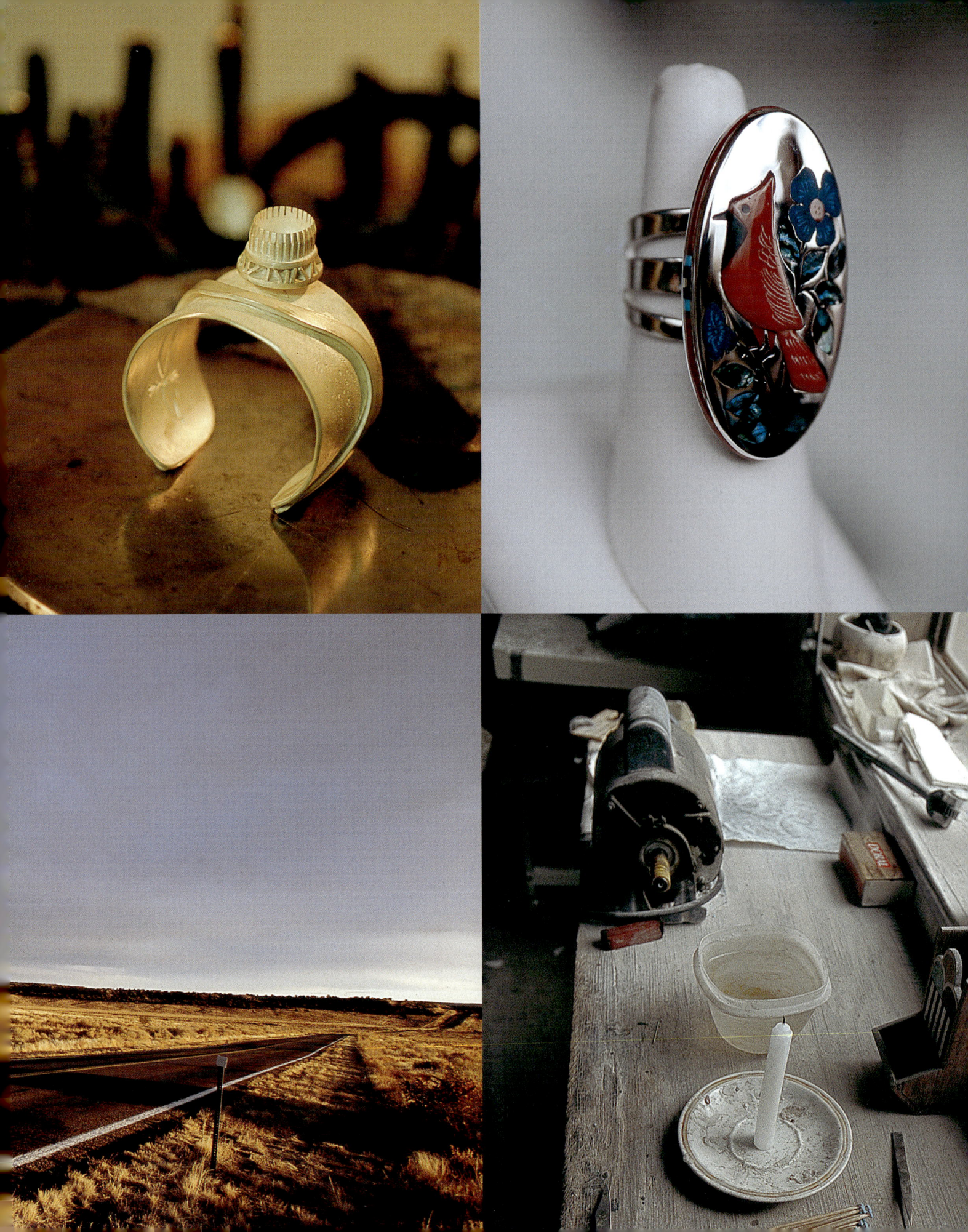

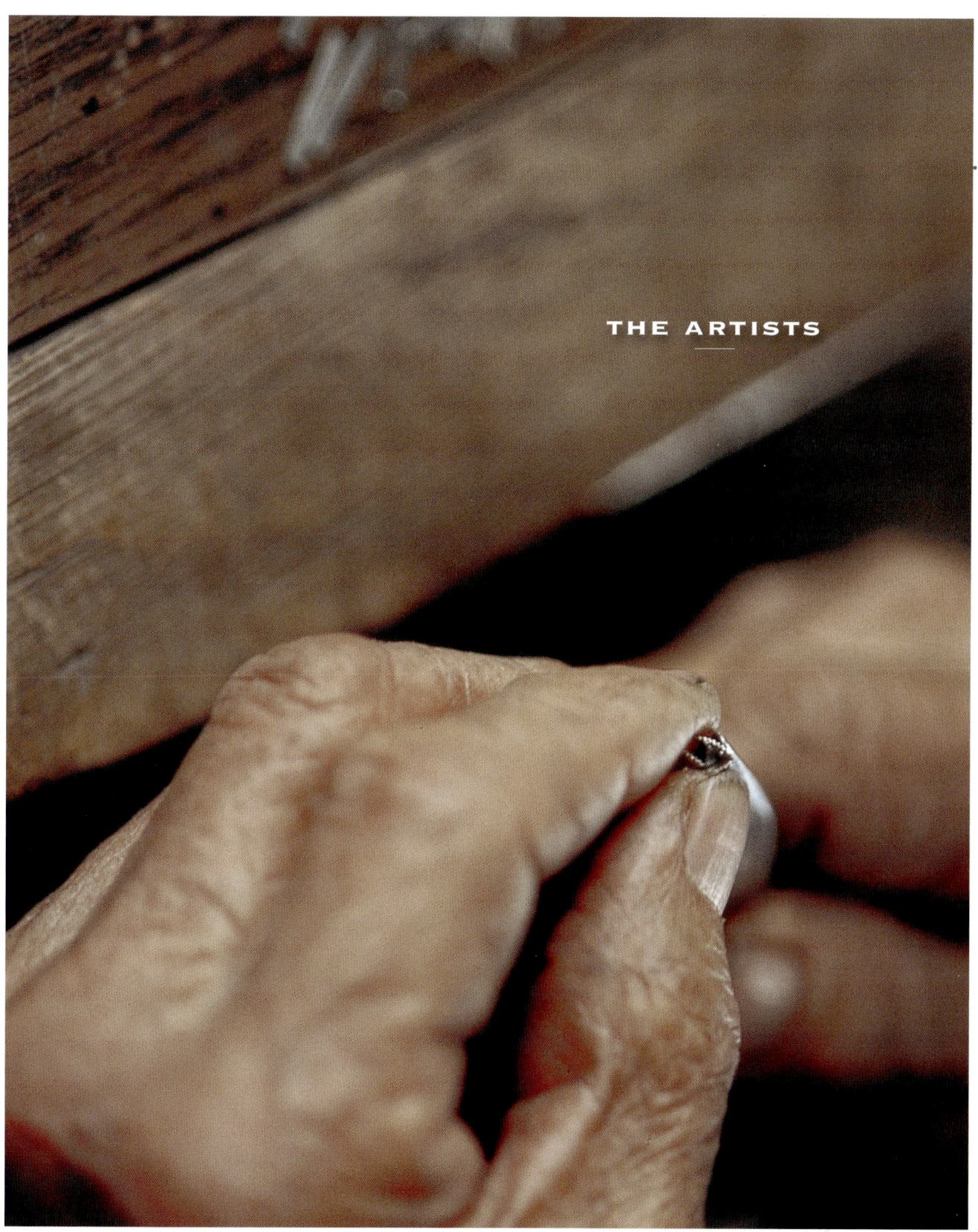

THE ARTISTS

OPPOSITE PAGE, CLOCKWISE FROM TOP LEFT: work of Michael Roanhorse Crawford, Jake Livingston, Bryant Waatsa.

ALEX BEESHLIGAII
NAVAJO

ALEX WAS BORN IN GANADO, ARIZONA, in 1953 to Roy Brown and Marie Elizabeth Wayne. He was born to the Grey Streak Mountain (Nihoobáanii) Clan and born for the Tsi'naajinii (Black-Streaked Wood) Clan. Alex's father and uncles did not work silver, but the generations before them did—all the way back to Atsidi Chon, one of the first Navajo silversmiths. Alex's mother was an artist in another medium, as a member of the Navajo singing group called the Klagetoh Maiden Singers. She recorded with Indian House records and, in a more traditional venue, was a singer of the Nightway chants—one of the many traditional healing ceremonies of the Navajos.

Of eight siblings, Alex is the only one working silver, having started learning the craft while attending Ganado High School. "I took one semester of art, and at the time I wasn't even interested in art," he says. "It was just a class I took." But this class was where he learned how to solder from the art teacher, a Hopi artist named Sherwood Numkema.

In 1976, while working on a BA in electrical engineering at Arizona State University in Tempe, Alex went to the Phoenix Indian Center, where he met the famed Navajo/Hopi jeweler Preston Monongye. Preston was teaching silversmithing classes at PIC as a part of the Jobs Training Partnership Act. Seeing Alex's potential, Preston tried to talk him out of school and into silversmithing. Alex kept up with his college studies (graduating in 1979), but he would sit in on the PIC classes.

Alex Beeshligaii with daughter, Denali, and son Taiyoni.

"After that I went to Alaska, in 1980. Juneau. I was eleven years up there, teaching, starting as a substitute teacher. Later I went into counseling minority kids, and about 1986 I moved to Anchorage and got training in special-ed classes at Alaska Pacific University." After that Alex was hired as a Native American studies instructor with Anchorage Unified School District, eventually moving back to the Southwest in 1991. While attending the University of Arizona, serving on the board of the Tucson Indian Center, and teaching, he continued making silver as a source of income and artistic expression. Alex also worked as an extra in movies filmed around southern Arizona, often helping with the casting of American Indian actors, and in the process meeting a number of American Indian artists—and his future wife, Lynn.

One of the artists he met was Allan Wallace (Washo-Maidu tribes), who taught Alex many of the finer points of silversmithing and introduced him to the art of inlaying stone and shell, a technique that has become something of a hallmark of Alex's work. Alex used to stop by and watch Allan at work until one day when Allan said to him, "You want to learn? Here're some stones …"

Remembers Alex, "I watched and learned by observing. I worked with him for about two years, learning inlay techniques as well as pricing, business conduct, the pros and cons of shows, and marketing. I'm always grateful that I met him and learned from him." Allan also took Alex along to his first retail show, in Litchfield Park, Arizona, where Alex began the practical application of what he had learned from Allan.

A couple of years later Alex began to do sand-cast work "to mix it up with the inlay. I was at a shop downtown [in Tucson] watching Alvin Thompson [Navajo] doing cement-and-oil casting, and I started thinking this would be cool to do. So after much trial and error I successfully cast a piece. I remembered watching Preston Monongye cast silver years ago, but actually doing it was a real experience." He laughs. "Allan would be watching and laughing. In time, though, I became pretty proficient at it." Using the cement-and-oil technique, Alex goes down to the arroyos (desert watercourses or gullies), gathering sand and sifting it three or four times to get a more consistent grade. He then mixes the sand with vegetable and canola oil, kneading it until it holds together and can be carved. Laughing, he recalls, "I tried using motor oil once … When I poured in the molten silver, the mold erupted in smoke and flame. Vegetal oil smells, but not as bad as engine oil!"

He also borrowed a roller and learned to melt his scrap silver into ingots and roll it out into sheet silver. This allowed him to experiment with overlay work. "Overlay I had seen in different places and all that, but it wasn't until I was introduced to Rick Manuel [see page 110] that I began to learn it. One summer—1995, I think—I hung out with him on a daily basis and watched him work. Three months. He's the one that kinda taught me about the metal itself, and different gauges. I watched him work, watched his cuts, saw how refined his work was, saw how to polish the final product without ruining the crisp edges. He uses different-size saw blades to make his cuts, his people, his plants. Everything comes alive in his work. So I observed that during that time."

Alex is the father of four boys and one girl. His oldest son, Warren, attends ASU. His next-eldest son, Shane (b. 1991), is now making some jewelry. Shane started learning from his dad at age nine and by thirteen could cut and polish stones, solder, tufa-cast, and roll sheet silver from ingot. Alex's other children, Kii, Taiyoni, and the littlest, daughter Denali, are still too young to begin—yet.

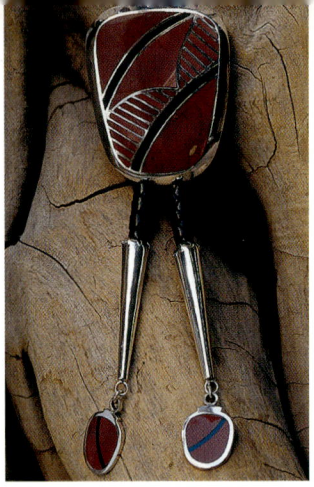

GEORGE AND DONNA BENNETT AND FAMILY

HAVASUPAI (GEORGE) AND ACOMA (DONNA)

GEORGE (OLIVER) BENNETT, A MEMBER OF THE HAVASUPAI TRIBE, was born in Seligman, Arizona, in 1944 to Lavonne Gonzales. He has led a varied and interesting life. "Out of high school I cowboyed for a while on the Diamond A [the Boquillas Ranch]," he says. "Then I went to Oklahoma State Tech in Okmulgee in 1965–66 to learn carpentry. Then I joined the Marine Corps in 67—my MOS was combat engineer. Got sent to Vietnam, Puerto Rico, and Camp Pendleton. After finishing my tour of duty in 1970 I applied for a job as behavioral consultant for Intermountain [Intermountain Center for Human Development] in Tucson. I really didn't expect to be hired, but they said, 'You start Monday.' It was a training and work program for kids that was started on Mt. Lemmon [in the Catalina Mountains immediately north of Tucson] by Dr. Giles. They closed the Mt. Lemmon part of the program in 1972, so I went back into carpentry and eventually full-time in jewelry when I got laid off from my carpentry job."

He became interested in jewelry as a kid, beginning when his grandma, Ruby Quasula, took him to the annual Fourth of July powwow in Flagstaff. "I ran around while she was busy gambling; Grandma used to win jewelry and stuff, like mutton. One time I watched this old Navajo guy painting and preaching. And when I went back the next day he was doing silversmithing and preaching. I had looked at the jewelry and wondered how they did it, so when I saw that Navajo man do it, it was, 'Wow!'"

His first foray into working silver came many years later, when he met Donna Sanchez, whom he would marry in 1976. Donna (b. 1951) was the daughter of Ethel Shields, a well-known potter from Acoma Pueblo. "Her stepdad used to brag about making gold rings," says George. "One day he brought home a silver platter and cut it up and made jewelry out of it. So I teased him: 'Oh, you weren't lying, you do make jewelry!' And I asked him to show me how. But he wouldn't, so I watched him for maybe two weeks and then

asked him if I could use his torch. He points at it and doesn't say anything. I didn't even know how to turn it on! He went out for a few minutes and when he came back he saw I just melted the silver, and he started laughing. But I kept trying and got the hang of it."

George started out selling his work at swap meets. "At first I made mostly rings that I sold at the De Anza Drive-In and Tanque Verde swap meets. Then, as I got better and made more types of things, I began entering jewelry shows. One dealer there said he liked it but said skeptically that it was 'too good to be made by you—Indian jewelry is not perfect; it has flaws.'"

George did not start off with a lot of equipment, and to say he is largely self-taught would be to put it mildly. "I started out doing lapidary work by filing the stones," he says. "This old guy saw me working at it during a show and started laughing and said, 'You know there is a better way, don't you?' I said, 'No.' He told me to get a grinding wheel." When George got into lost-wax casting in the 1980s, he made his own vacuum caster out of a refrigerator motor that he reversed. "Then I bought a real one," he smiles.

"I learned as I did repairs, and some of what I learned came as a surprise. I was fixing a piece of jewelry for a lady—a coral stone was missing. When I got it home and looked at the other stones I saw they weren't stones, they were beans painted with red nail polish!" he recalls, laughing. A quick learner, by his second year he was making difficult reversible necklaces that were winning prizes.

Wife Donna, whose sister Charmae Natseway is a well-known potter like their mother, is the only family member in her generation currently working silver. She met George at the Tucson Indian Center, where her mother was a summer cook. Donna taught swimming, and George was working there as well. Donna has been a teacher for the past nineteen years, having earned a bachelor's in special education from the University of Arizona, followed by a master's in language, reading, and culture in 1997.

She started out by doing the buffing and polishing for George's work. As important as it is to the final product, the job is dirty and demanding. It was not long before Donna said, "Forget this, I'll do my *own* work!" Like her husband, she is largely self-taught. She makes mostly earrings, set with small cut stones. "I specialize in inlay work but with a different color palette than most [jewelry artists]," she says. And she adds, "My work is not as heavy as George's." Her work has won ribbons, including at Santa Fe Indian Market.

Now their sons are working silver. Robert Eli (b. 1976) and Ethaniel George (b. 1978) started learning while still in elementary school and were entering their work in shows and winning ribbons by middle school. Ethaniel is particularly noted for his fine and intricate handmade chains. With the world just beginning to unfold before them, whether they will pursue jewelry as a career is something only time will tell. What is certain is that they could not have had better, more resourceful teachers.

ROLAND BRADY
NAVAJO

DUE TO TIME CONSTRAINTS, my initial interview with Roland Brady was over the phone. It was a short call, as he was in the middle of frying up some chicken wings, and then he was going to have to go get the sheep and bring them in to the pen for the night. He said he'd call me back the next day.

When he called back, the sheep were out grazing, and he had time to talk about his work and his life. He was born in 1963 in Shiprock, New Mexico, a community named for a 1,700-foot-tall volcanic plug that sits prominently on the horizon; the Navajos call it Tse'bi t'ai, or Rock Wings. According to Navajo religion, it is the remains of marauding monster birds killed by the Navajo Warrior Twins.

The son of Marlene Benally and Andrew Brady, Roland was born and raised on Dinetah (Navajoland); he went to high school in Kayenta, a Navajo town about two hours west of Shiprock. One of his memories from that time is a field trip during which he had the opportunity to see and study Van Gogh's painting *Starry Night*. It was from his mother that he learned silversmithing, a craft she had learned while attending Santa Fe Indian School (which later became the Institute of American Indian Art). "I used to sit next to her and watch, and she'd guide my hand with the torch to teach me soldering when I was maybe eight," he recalls. "I started with making rings and kind of progressed from there."

He gave it up when he went away to college at Northern Arizona University in Flagstaff, where he started in the pre-engineering program, later transferring to the

University of Arizona in Tucson. It was there, at the Center for Creative Photography, that he first saw and was impressed by Ansel Adams's work. But engineering lost its hold on him, and "after three years I pretty much quit. I came home and attended community college at Kayenta, taking some classes with Shonto Begay [a well-known Navajo artist and author]. I'd always been drawing, as long as I can remember. I learned to work in oils and experimented with pointillism and pen-and-ink work."

During this time he supported himself as a tour guide, a connection he made courtesy of a college roommate who worked for a company that ran tours out of Kayenta into Monument Valley. "My roommate didn't have any time to drive one summer, so I filled in. I started driving for Bill Crawley [the tour company operator], driving up to Monument Valley three times a day for a whole year. And I just fell in love with the place and the wildlife. From there I began working for Cisco's Location Services and was a location guide for the next fifteen years." Monument Valley, in Navajo called Tse'bíí Ndzísgaíí (Valley of the Rocks), is a place of such compelling beauty that it captivates all who visit, including the Navajo guides themselves. Roland spent every spare moment sketching the valley, which twenty years later has lost none of its magical appeal for him.

In his capacity as location guide he has been on a Travel Channel segment of *Stranded with Cash Peters* and was also involved in the production of the movie *Into the West* as a location guide, extra, and stand-in. "It was a sad story, but I was glad to be able to help with the visual part. And I met a lot of interesting folks."

It was a busy, rewarding life. But "my silver tools were just sitting here for so long they were covered with dust. Out of boredom or need to create, I started messing around, making some jewelry. I got a lot of good feedback, so I entered the Heard Museum show in

1999, and there I met other artists and dealers, including Susan Garland, and later Wayne Bobrick. They really boosted me, reaffirmed my work. I am indebted to them."

Roland is the great-grandson of Tsí ísh bízhí, or Braided Hair, the man who gave land to the Franciscans for their now-historic mission at St. Michaels, Arizona, just west of Window Rock, the Navajo Nation's capital. Braided Hair was given the English name Paul Brady and was baptized a Catholic, a faith Roland and his family still follow. Much of Roland's work (which recently expanded to include unique rosaries) includes cross imagery that ranges from X-like figures that some might identify as star motifs to the double-barred crosses that the early Pueblo silversmiths interpreted as dragonfly motifs. He has studied the silver crosses in museum collections, in old jewelry cases in galleries, and in books on the subject, but his cross imagery is uniquely his own and has taken a very baroque turn. He also finds inspiration in the designs found on ancient potsherds, incorporating them into bracelets that have designs hidden on the inside. Most of his work is in plain silver with gold accents, and his subject matter ranges from crosses to plant and insect motifs, all with his hand-finishing. "I polish by hand and use emery cloth to give the silver that luxurious, melty look," he says. "Polishing by hand is time-consuming, but it is better for the integrity of the piece. In accordance with Dineh [Navajo] tradition, all my work retains a mark of incompletion to maintain balance and *hozho* [a Navajo word usually translated as "beauty," but it means more—encompassing a sense of harmony and balance]. This is achieved by simply omitting or changing the size of a design." He adds, "Nature—the cosmos entity—is the only complete and therefore perfect reality."

JOSEPH AND MARY CALABAZA AND FAMILY
SANTO DOMINGO PUEBLO

JOSEPH (B. 1946) AND MARY (B. 1949) both come from families with long histories of working in shell and stone. Joseph was born an only child to Patricio (Pat) and Caroline Calabaza. Pat started his selling and trading career as a young boy, going to the railroad station or the highway to sell the pottery his mother made. Pat lived with his son and daughter-in-law after his wife died but continued hitchhiking around, selling shell and stone necklaces, or *heishe,* until well into his eighties. He died at age eighty-six, still working at his craft and planning yet another selling trip.

A certified welder, Joseph started learning heishe making by helping his father. "He used to make a little heavier pieces; I went into finer," he says. "I started when I was about sixteen and worked into finer work in my twenties." He met Mary in the 1960s, marrying her in 1969. "She encouraged me to do finer work. So we both started on the finer together."

Mary's parents, Victor and Ramona Tenorio, had three sons and six daughters, all of whom helped their parents make *joclas* (a style of necklace that has a dangling ornament that might otherwise be used as an earring), selling to folks in Albuquerque, Santa Fe, and the pueblos along the Rio Grande. Her father spoke Navajo and traded with Navajo families living in the area around Crownpoint, a hundred miles or so northwest of the pueblo. Mary learned the basics from her parents, but she credits Joseph's father with teaching her the more advanced techniques.

When it came to fine heishe, however, there was really no one to teach them. In this new area they were largely self-taught, experimenting and inventing as they went along. Unable to find the right-size drill bit for their new, finer work, they figured out how to make one. The drill tip was fitted to an old-style pump drill, which they continued to use until 1978 when they found an electric drill that was suitable. (Shell and turquoise will heat up, crack, and even burn if drilled at high speeds, so for many traditionally trained bead-makers, the pump drill continued in use until electric drills, with better rheostats to manage the speed, became affordable and available.)

They began showing their new, finer work at shows in Santa Fe, the Heard Museum, then Indianapolis and Pasadena. Once it was seen, orders began coming in from across the nation, from California to New York. In the thirty-five years since their first appearance, shows have continued to be an important part of their business; it's the way they have met many of the retailers who handle their work as well as the collectors who cherish it.

They started with shell, turquoise, and jet, later adding coral, fossilized ivory, serpentine, lapis, and, before the 1972 Endangered Species Act banned it, hawksbill tortoiseshell. The loss of the latter material was keenly felt, as tortoiseshell was best suited for creating the finest heishe made—as small as 8/10 of a millimeter in diameter (for comparison, most heishe is strung on thread that is 6/10 of a millimeter). At such fineness, they needed to string fifty strands in order to have enough "visual weight" to be seen and appreciated. To create such fine beads in stone means to be very fussy about the quality of the materials in terms of hardness, matrix, and absence of fracture lines. By 1980 they were starting to mix different-color materials in their necklaces, and added silver and gold accents.

They have four sons, Joe Ralph, Joe Allan, Aldon, and Irvin, and one daughter, DeAlva. All started out helping their parents with the family business at an early age. Says Mary, "We started them at about five years old, having them help us put the bead blanks on wire. We had them count the beads—450 per strand; we don't count them anymore. They follow our design style, especially our daughter. She is very creative, and she works in silver and makes our silver cones, too."

Their children have carried their parents' drive for excellence in heishe to the educational arena. Daughter DeAlva went to the University of New Mexico, starting out pre-law and earning a master's in business. The sons have gone into business, administration, and accounting. Jonathan Calabaza, the oldest of their eleven grandchildren, was awarded a Gates Millennium Scholarship, as well as earning the Wheelwright Museum's Goodman Fellowship, and now attends the University of Arizona, where he is considering a career as a pediatrician. And among those carrying the family tradition of fine heishe into the twenty-first century is their oldest granddaughter, Tiffany (b. 1989), who has begun making and designing her own work. Currently Mary's granddaughters Valerie, age eight, Briana and Ramona, both age seven, and Onika, age six, are happily learning the craft from their grandmother.

MICHAEL AND MARK ROANHORSE CRAWFORD
NAVAJO

IF YOU RUN INTO MICHAEL AT AN INDIAN ART SHOW, the first thing you'll notice is his height: six foot three. But as you draw closer to his booth, it is the distinctive silver and gold work of Michael and his brother Mark that will capture your attention and captivate you.

Born to the Kin yaa'áanii (Towering House) Clan and for the Tóbaahí (Water's Edge) Clan in 1975 to Georgia White and Eugene Crawford Jr., Michael and his siblings—older brother Duane, younger brother Mark (b. 1985), and sisters Yvonne and Taina—grew up in Crystal, New Mexico, where high grazing lands and alfalfa fields meet the dark forests of the western slopes of the Chuska Mountains. Theirs is a ranch and rodeo family whose patriarch, Eugene Crawford Sr., is one of the honored Navajo Marine Code Talkers from World War II. The family name Crawford came about when someone (not a family member and not Navajo) decided that his great-great-grandfather's name, which translates as Roanhorse, ought to be changed to something English. In light of this, Michael is planning on a new hallmark for his work, Michael Roanhorse, reclaiming a traditional family name.

All five children learned silversmithing from their father, who had once traveled widely, making and selling sand-cast squash-blossom necklaces and concha belts set with large-nugget turquoise. Eugene showed his silverwork at the Santa Fe Indian Market about 1970; he was also an accomplished leather worker. At one point, during the boom period of the mid-1970s, he had a workshop in Gallup where as many as five Navajo silversmiths executed his designs. He still occasionally makes jewelry.

OPPOSITE PAGE, TOP LEFT & RIGHT: Mark Roanhorse Crawford; BOTTOM LEFT & ABOVE: Work of Michael Roanhorse Crawford.

Michael graduated from high school in Gallup in 1994, after which he moved to Albuquerque to attend the city's Technical Vocational Institute (TVI), where he earned certification as an independent electrical contractor in 2000.

While attending school four days a week, he commuted home to Crystal to work silver on the weekends in a small wooden building built by Michael and his father and used by the family as a workshop. Their father had moved on to found a construction company in 1984, leaving the jewelry business to his three sons. It was about this time that Michael began learning and perfecting his silversmithing skills and began to develop his unique style, with his father instructing him in many of the finer points.

During this time youngest brother Mark watched his older brothers at work and observed carefully and patiently. Recalls Michael, "Mark was nine then, when he was watching us work. He started out helping our older brother, Duane. He was very curious and would watch us all the time."

As Mark tells it, "After casting there would be bits of silver here and there that Duane would collect to use for the next casting, but there were always a few tiny scraps that he overlooked. I would pick up all the little scraps and put them into a coffee can. After a couple months I had enough to cast. I carved a mold for a *ketoh* [bowguard] and got ready to cast it. Duane watched to make sure I wasn't going to burn the place down." And the bowguard, set with turquoise, came out so beautifully that it would do credit to any seasoned silversmith, let alone a nine-year-old.

Recalling that first piece of jewelry, Mark smilingly reveals that when helping pour the molten silver for his brothers' work he would occasionally make sure there was a small spill to help build his scrap-silver supply. His father was the one who showed him how to carve volcanic tuff for sand-cast work, and it quickly became evident to the rest of the family that he had a gift for it. "From there they discovered I was the best caster—so I'd cast their orders, and then they would do all the stonesetting and finishing."

In 1995, at age twenty, Michael took his own work out to sell, going to Santa Fe, where his works, mostly conchas, were turned down by shop after shop until the Brown Cow Saddle Blanket Company bought them and ordered silver-mounted horse bridles, giving him his first show in 1998.

Meanwhile, younger brother Mark was diligently working at developing his own silversmithing skills and style and going to school. While a freshman at St. Michaels High School, he entered an exceptional piece in a competition in Gallup called Reunion of the Masters Show, garnering a prize. In his senior year of high school he cast a sculpture in pieces, soldered them together, then inlaid the base with turquoise, coral, lapis, and gold. He called it *Yei'ii Corn God,* and in the 2004 Heard Museum Show, student division, it won best in classification, best in division, and best of show. In all, Mark earned twelve ribbons that year, eleven for this sculpture.

Michael Roanhorse Crawford.

Work of Mark Roanhorse Crawford.

As with the bowguard years earlier, he had set a goal for himself and patiently, diligently set about achieving it. "After I cast the pieces and saw how it was turning out, I decided to go for the best-of-show award. I added inlay work to the base, then also incorporated gold for the eyes, mouth, and other body parts, and added stones."

Michael, who was working silver to pay his bills while attending school, says that younger brother Mark inspired him and encouraged him, saying, "Don't worry about the money part, worry about succeeding as an artist with your own vision." And so, beginning in the early 1990s, he shifted the vision of his work to a more contemporary, personal style.

In 2004, the two brothers had their first booth at the Santa Fe Indian Market (though they had entered work in the show in 2002), and their work gained a new and appreciative audience. They also found mentors, fellow silversmiths who advised them, including Arlan Ben, Ric Charlie, and Vernon Hoskie.

Michael now also has a workshop space in Albuquerque, so he no longer commutes to Crystal. Attending TVI, where he majors in construction management and technology with an electrical emphasis, he is also working on a degree at the University of New Mexico in business with a minor in marketing—a twenty-first-century version of his father's entrepreneurial model.

In keeping with that, his buffer, lapidary equipment, and torch share space with a digital camera and Internet-connected computer with which he does his own photographs, brochures, and marketing—which he works on during the day, along with his schoolwork. Like many silversmiths, he prefers to work on his jewelry in the evenings. "I forget about time, about eating … everything but work." He often works until the predawn light begins to silhouette the Sandia Mountains and a new piece of jewelry literally sees the first light of day.

Michael's son Michael Jr. was born in 1994. His work earned first-, second-, and third-prize ribbons for stampwork bracelets (youth division) in 2003 at the Wheelwright Museum in Santa Fe. Michael Jr. gave one bracelet to each of his grandmothers and sold the third.

Mark was born in Phoenix, prematurely. "I wanted to get an early start," he smiles, a statement that seems plausible, given his nature and his accomplishments. But problems

Michael Roanhorse Crawford.

Mark Roanhorse Crawford.

stemmed from his early arrival. "When I was younger they wanted to do brain surgery, but my family used traditional ceremonies instead to get through it and it turned out okay." Those traditions continue to see the family through when a crisis arises.

Mark's original plans were to attend Thunderbird International Business School in Phoenix, go to Germany, and learn how to cut and set stones while there. Instead he finally chose Northern Arizona University, where he is majoring in art management and "would like to open a gallery, maybe down in Sedona, and later on in the future create a scholarship to help Native American youth as well. Maybe establish an art show for youth and emerging artists." Ambitious plans, but they come from a young man with an impressive track record.

Michael plans to use his degree in business and marketing as a complement to his art career, which he sees as expanding to include stone and metal sculpture. It is already apparent from his jewelry that he is combining sculpture and jewelry into a style uniquely his own. He has also thought about someday opening a gallery in Santa Fe to showcase the work of emerging artists. "There are a lot of young artists out there that have the talent but don't know how to get their foot in the door," he says. "They just need a little help, a little guidance on the business side of starting out."

Mark and Michael—each with his own artistic vision, plans for the future, and considerable talent—will do well, in large measure because they are armed with the values instilled in them by their supportive family.

BERNARD DAWAHOYA
HOPI

BERNARD DAWAHOYA IS A REMARKABLE MAN. Born to the Snow Clan in 1937, he never had a formal education and learned English only as an adult, yet his impact on his community has been exceptional. Roughly thirty Hopi silversmiths, many of them quite famous, began as his students, and all I have spoken with hold him in high esteem.

When Bernard was a young boy, his parents sent him from his home village of Songoopavi off to work for his uncle, Sidney Secakuku, and a clan relative, Washington Talayumptewa. Leaving his three brothers and three sisters behind, the little boy headed some miles south of Second Mesa with his uncles. (In Hopi kinship, male and female members of one's clan are addressed as uncles and aunts.) Both men were well-known silversmiths, but the help they wanted was for something other than silverworking. "I watched the sheep while they worked the silver. Later I was the motor for the grinder," he laughs. "They used to make squash blossoms [for trade]. I used to watch them, and then one time I borrowed their tools to try it. They caught me and decided to put me to work on silver."

The men made their jewelry using silver coins, slugs, and old spoons. Melting them down and hammering them out was a long, demanding, and tedious task, so once, on a trip to Winslow, they tried a different approach. As Bernard tells it, "One time they took me to [Winslow] to sell [jewelry and katsina dolls] to the people that come on the train and that have cars. When we got there we tied coins on to the track and waited for the train. It flattened out the coins *real good*."

In time Bernard learned more typical silverworking techniques, including how to set stones. He had time to devote to livestock and silverwork because "I never went to school, you know, and when I was growing up the school wants me to come and I don't want to because I'm all black from the sun. But then I guess Washington [Talayumptewa] and my uncle got rid of the sheep [apparently due to Navajo encroachment on Hopi grazing lands south of the mesas] and then I got no job. I come to the village and I hardly know *anybody* here because I was at sheep camp all that time. So one time I decided to go and try school anyway. I was there with the little ones and so after two or three days I quit."

After being initiated into the Katsina society, he began to work silver for a living. "Uncle let me use his tools for a while, but then I start collecting my own tools. Later [starting in the 1960s] I had calls from different people to demonstrate—in Flagstaff, Heard, Gallup, Albuquerque, Santa Fe."

He and his wife, Alice, have been married for many years, a marriage that began with their parents' arrangement. "They put us together so we got married. She's the one that went to school. She teaches me English—when to say yes or no," he smiles. Together they have raised two daughters.

There is a long tradition of entrepreneurship at Hopi, and Bernard is an important part of it. He opened his own silversmithing shop in 1960—one of the first such shops. It was there that he started teaching silver; among some of his better-known students are Glenn Lucas, Weaver Selina, and Phillip Honanie.

His clan uncle Talayumptewa worked extensively with turquoise and shell, carving fetishes and making mosaics he set in silver. Bernard tried it, but after winding up once with a piece of stabilized turquoise (one impregnated with a plastic resin to harden it), he "decided to quit fooling around with that—what was the need of turquoise?"

He started selling his work at shows beginning in the 1950s and traveled widely, selling in Flagstaff, Phoenix, Tucson, Los Alamos, Holbrook, and Taos. Now collectors and shop owners alike must seek him out at his shop just outside Songoopavi Village, or rely upon the mail.

A modest, self-effacing man, he says, "Mostly I pick up my designs from broken potteries; they have nice designs on them." He adds, "I learn a lot from you people. I talk to people at the shows to learn what it is that they really want." Despite the modesty, his silversmithing excellence has not gone unnoticed. In 1989, "They told me 'You better come down. We have something to give you'. So I went down there." What they had for him "down there" (Phoenix) was the honor of being named an Arizona Living Treasure. Now seventy, he can still be found behind his workbench in his old shop at the entrance to the village.

DENNIS AND NANCY EDAAKIE AND FAMILY
ZUNI

OPPOSITE PAGE: Dale Edaakie.

BELOW: Dennis Edaakie.

FOR MORE THAN A HALF-CENTURY, the Edaakie family has been creating some of the most admired jewelry to come out of Zuni. Dennis, born to the Parrot Clan in 1931, and Nancy, born into the Frog Clan in 1937, create a type of inlay jewelry in which the design is cut out of one sheet of silver and overlaid onto another solid sheet. Then the recessed area is set or inlaid with stone and shell.

Nancy did not begin making jewelry until after she and Dennis were married (in 1954, after he got back from Korea and out of the Army), but Dennis started as a young boy, watching his uncle, Jake Haloo Sr. "I just watched him do his type of work," he says. "I had this feeling that if he can do it I can do it better. And I did—eventually! I started a long time ago. I was going to school then—I was fifteen years old. Me and my older sister, Elizabeth, were making inlay work. We sold to Vanderwagen and C. G. Wallace. But we didn't do the silver settings. They had Navajos do that."

It was from his father, Merle, that he learned inlay work. Along with his brothers—Theodore, Lee, and Anthony—Merle made some of the finest inlay and mosaic work in Zuni. If the family name seems tricky to spell, take comfort in the fact that official records vary in their spelling. In the Zuni language the name is *Idak kai ye*. Government officials thought that sounded like Edaaki, which somehow later became Edaakie.

"I learned inlay work from my dad, Merle," says Dennis. "The hardest thing is the first time you try something new. It's always the hardest time. The first time, I didn't know how

to cut it out. See, what I did was I tried it out on copper plate. I bought a copper plate. I practiced on it. Later on I used silver. I started silverwork full-time in 1964. At the time I was working at the truck stop in Gallup. At that time they were working on I-40. When they finished it the station lost business and shut down—in January 1964. And that is when I started to make jewelry full-time.

"I was doing knifewing and rainbow, thunderbird, and sunface designs. I started out making those four designs. We made whatever we made and took it over there [to traders Vanderwagen or C. G. Wallace]. We got half cash and half due bill [trade credit]."

Along the way he began selling some of his work to Leon and Ruth Ingram of Gallup. "They were the sort of people who expected us to bring in different kinds of jewelry. It was their idea that I make something that had never been made before to enter in Ceremonial [the Gallup Intertribal Ceremonial, established in 1926]. It was Ruth that came up with the idea. She was going through pages of this magazine, saw a cardinal and asked us about it. I said, 'I'll try,' and she said, 'If you make one we'll enter it!' I came home, made a sketch, and tried it. I tried using red abalone, then pipestone, but it didn't work out. Finally I tried coral. It took first place."

By then, Nancy was actively involved in creating work with her husband. "When I got into birds she was doing the flowers and leaves and stuff like that. Later on she learned to make birds." The hallmark changed to reflect this—from the parrot-beak hallmark (1965), then DENNIS E (around 1970), and finally DENNIS AND NANCY EDAAKIE (from about 1983 on).

A year after that first cardinal pendant came a new innovation. "Ruth again—she would come up with these ideas—she asked me if I could make a reversible pendant. She promised to enter it again. It took me a while to figure out how I would make it reversible without having to take it off to show the other side. Finally I came up with a swivel design. I switched from flat to domed pendants a little while after that. I thought it might be a lot better if I make them domed. The borders came that first year, too." Nancy noted that other ideas suggested by Ruth included hummingbird and apple blossoms. Koshare (Pueblo clown) designs came in the 1970s, when the owner of a shop of the same name requested one. Dennis was quickly approached by others who wanted jewelry with that design. Ever respectful, Dennis recounted, "When someone else saw it and asked for one I had to ask her permission to use it—it was her logo." Unfortunately, others have not been so respectful, shamelessly copying his designs to the smallest detail. "It used to bother me a lot. But later on I just let it go," he says. It should be noted, however, that no one who copies comes close to the quality workmanship of Dennis and Nancy.

They have five children—two daughters (one teaching, one currently working at Wal-Mart) and three sons. All three sons, Dale (formerly known as Myron), Derrick, and Sanford, work silver in the general style of their parents. Sanford (b. 1963) started working silver when he was twenty, after being laid off from a job he had started the year before. His work—largely earrings and pin-pendants, though occasionally larger pieces—focuses on animals, birds, and the occasional frog. Derrick (b. 1965) works in a similar style, having also learned from his parents. Dale (b. 1957) began jewelry-making when he was twenty-one. He generally employs designs of animals, explaining, "I usually leave the birds for my brothers and my folks to do—I'm more of a wildlife artist." But he has been known to branch out and create some very unusual work. When one dealer, Martha Struever of Santa Fe, received a cartoon depicting the Wicked Witch of the West decked out in Western attire and Indian jewelry, she was so taken with it that she asked Dale if he could create something inspired by that concept. He did, and then, in the same vein, made a series of jack-o-lantern pin pendants, set with orange spondylus shell. Each one is unique, as he varies the designs.

Dennis and Nancy have never kept any of their own work, though Dennis tried once. "I made a gold bola tie with a parrot. It was supposed to be my own personal bola tie. But at a hotel in Scottsdale I was wearing that parrot bola. These people came in and wanted to see my bolas, and I showed them my work; eagles, ducks, and all kinds, but they keep looking at my bola. Then they go outside and then come back in. This one man, he must have been from Texas because he had this big hat, he said, 'I want the bola.' 'Which one?' 'That one, I want that bola.' So I sold him my gold parrot bola tie."

Dennis and Nancy may not have kept any of their own work from over the years, but many grateful and appreciative collectors have—and have collected that of their children as well.

Sanford Edaakie.

CHEYENNE HARRIS
NAVAJO

PUSHED BY THE RELOCATION program established after World War II, and by economic opportunities in urban areas and increasing demographic pressures on-reservation, two-thirds of all Indians now live off-reservation, with an ever-increasing percentage also born off-reservation. Cheyenne Harris, born in Phoenix in 1963, is a member of that generational shift.

Her mother, Roberta Multine, earned a degree in elementary education from Arizona State University, teaching back home on the Navajo Reservation—first at the Rough Rock Demonstration School and Shiprock Elementary before accepting a teaching position at Phoenix Indian School and later at the Salt River (Pima) Day School. Cheyenne's father, George Harris Jr., a member of the Northern Cheyenne tribe, served in the Marine Corps, and passed away when Cheyenne was quite young.

Cheyenne's mother, who grew up near Low Mountain, Arizona, learned basic silversmithing skills from her father, Oscar Multine, and her grandfather, Henry Yazzie. While teaching at nearby Rough Rock Demonstration School in 1968, she refined her skills, studying silversmithing with the famed Kenneth Begay at Navajo Community College. It was a skill she relied on to help make ends meet in supporting her family, which grew to include three daughters.

Cheyenne in turn learned from her mother to love silver and work silver. She sold some work, mostly rings and earrings, during high school, selling primarily to the prestigious Heard Museum gift shop, then run by Byron Hunter Jr., whose father had bought work from her mother years earlier. Graduating from Mesa High in 1981, Cheyenne struck out on her own, heading to Flagstaff to attend Northern Arizona University. While there, she studied jewelry under Joe Coronet, took a workshop from the Korean jewelry artist Cornelia Okim, and earned a BFA. Those studies, however, were interrupted in 1983 when her mother passed away. Cheyenne returned to Phoenix to help her two younger half-sisters with the traumatic transition. A year later she returned to complete her degree at NAU, this time carrying with her the silversmithing tools she inherited from her mother, including a Sears hand drill and a bench pin that she still uses.

After completion of her undergraduate work at NAU she was accepted into Arizona State University's MFA program in jewelry, taking classes in architecture, interior design, and furniture along the way. In the midst of her graduate studies she took a year off and went to Santa Fe to teach at the famous Institute of American Indian Art. A terrible car accident seriously injured her back and brought an end to her graduate work at ASU. With a determination that has marked her life, she decided to begin working full-time as a self-employed jewelry artist.

While studying jewelry at the Haystack Mountain School of Crafts in Maine, she met Tony Abeyta, a well-known painter from a family of respected artists. He encouraged her to enter the Santa Fe Indian Market, which she did in 1987. To this day she sells much of her work through shows like Indian Market and at the Heard.

An admirer of the work of Arthur Stone (an English silversmith active in the early 1900s), she has created hollowware work and made sterling flatware. Currently she finds she is working more in gold (a material her mother also used) than silver, though she also creates mixed-media work—gold on silver and silver on gold—and is constantly experimenting with new design ideas, new stones, and new techniques.

FERDINAND AND SYLVIA HOOEE
ZUNI

FERDINAND, THE OLDEST OF SEVEN BROTHERS AND SISTERS (one a potter), was born in 1957. Sylvia, born Sylvia Tsethlikai in 1958, is also from a family of seven brothers and sisters (two of whom make petit-point jewelry and one of whom, Yolanda, is profiled on page 130). Ferdinand and Sylvia married young, out of the house by sixteen. They have a son, Alonzo, a daughter, Sherrie, and two grandchildren, Kimberly and Austin.

Ferdinand's stepfather, Lyqatie Laate, was a forest ranger, and his mother, Etta Lynn, made jewelry, and so it was from her that he and his siblings learned silverworking. "This was probably about 1972–73," Ferdinand says. "I started working in simple things. The first design I made—I can't take all the credit … my mother was there to help me—was a horseshoe-shaped pendant with three stones hanging from it. This was when I was about in the ninth grade. After school I would go home and sit next to her at the table and she would scold me and tell me to make something rather than sitting there wasting my time, so she helped me design and make it. I made something like a dollar a pendant. At the beginning she soldered for me until I got good at it. She was very patient with me, 'cause I did make a lot of mistakes. The hardest thing was the shaping of the metal [bezels] and then the soldering, 'cause I was always in a hurry. Out of ten bezels, six or seven would be good enough to finish. The rest just melted into what I called 'frustration balls.'

"Once I was cutting some sheet for earrings, using some sheet silver from the workbench drawer. I was preparing ten pair of earrings. I started soldering but nothing would

solder, nothing, no matter how carefully I tried. When my mother came home she saw what I was doing wrong, and she started laughing—I was using sheet solder, not sheet silver. I got more into it when they bought a motorcycle for me, and I had to pay for some of it. So that was when I *really* started.

"All us kids started out making [silver] drops [Mom] used in her jewelry. She made us line them up in a row to make beadwire. I don't know how many thousand drops we must have made. A while back I bought some manufactured beadwire, but I got to feeling so guilty that I didn't use it. It's still bundled up over there in my scrap can."

Sylvia's story is not unlike that of her husband; she, too, began silverworking when she was in the ninth grade. From her parents, Juan and Lyla Tsethlikai, she learned the demanding and delicate technique known as petit-point. "I started out with petit-point work, but mostly working only when I needed money for something," she says. "In the business it was mostly around ceremonial time [the Gallup Intertribal Ceremonial] when we got our money. We did beadwork jewelry and figures as well."

From Sylvia's early sales at Ceremonial and Ferdinand's first sales at Turquoise Village in Zuni, they began to wholesale to a wide range of dealers. They never considered selling direct until one fateful day in 1993 in Zuni when they "saw a big sign outside the tribal office that said something like 'Get more money for your jewelry!'" They wound up joining the Zuni Cultural Arts Council started by Tony and Carlton Jamon and attending workshops at the middle school on how to price and market their work direct. Years later they laughingly recall their first day selling retail at a small show: "We were scared to death! But we wound up doing really good. We were so surprised. We didn't sell as many pieces as when we wholesaled, but we still made more money." Finally, in 1999 they opened their shop, Silver Rain Jewelry. That day in April they were up early and very nervous. "We hardly got any customers at first." But success has followed their perseverance and willingness to take a chance.

One thing that has not changed is their commitment to the quality of their work and the importance of the design process. Says Ferdinand, "I always drew on scraps of paper, paper bags. All the time. It turned out that Sylvia had been saving them. I was surprised; I thought they had all been thrown away. We have a thick folder of designs. We started out with the stars-and-feathers design, but I will look at something and see a design and right away get a pencil and paper. Anything handy. I'm not an artist who can draw. I can't make it exactly the way I see it in my head, but when I work in silver I can." Their drawings are largely geometric: "We never draw, or make use of, katsina designs. For us personally it is a taboo."

They prefer to work late at night, starting after dinner and sometimes going until first light. "We get more done that way—no interruptions. We listen to the TV, but if I watch it I won't get anything done. Usually we just listen to music: oldies, country, and powwow."

They sell at more than a dozen shows each year: Litchfield, Arizona; Arizona State Museum in Tucson; Heard Museum; Eiteljorg Museum; Jemez Pueblo; Eight Northern Pueblos; Zuni Expo; Sharlot Hall; Museum of Northern Arizona; Lawrence (Kansas); Dallas; and Mesa Southwest Museum. And in between those shows, at some of the feast days at the pueblos.

Despite such a schedule, they insist, "We are slowing down a little now; in the beginning we could do twenty-five pair of our star earrings in a week. That would be impossible now, but being able to sell retail has been a big change, a big improvement." The "slowing down" may have more than a little to do with the exceptional level of craftsmanship they have achieved in their work. As a reminder, they have saved the first star bracelet they made so many years ago. "Occasionally we take it out to look at it—and laugh at it."

JACKSON FAMILY
NAVAJO

IN TRADITIONAL NAVAJO LIFE you acquire your mother's clan (known as your "born to" clan) and your father's clan ("born for" clan). Gene Jackson's "born to" clan is Kin yaa'áanii (Towering House) and his "born for" clan is Tó dích'íi'nii (Bitterwater), and he was born in Jeddito, Arizona, to Bernice Charlie and John Nez Begay. That much is certain. What is not certain is the year of his birth: it was between 1930 and 1933, depending upon whom or whose records you choose to believe. The Social Security Administration picked 1933 and that suits Gene. Those same records pick the month variously as December, January, and May. Since his family told him he was born in the fall, Gene chose a date in October as his birthday. And like many Navajos, he started life with a Navajo name but wound up being given an English name (Jackson, in his case) by a system that could not handle the Navajo language. He has four brothers—Dan, Benson, Johnny, and Henry—all of whom work silver.

The birth date of Gene's wife, Martha, 1936, is more certain. Her born-to clan is Bit'ahnii (Folding Arms) and her born-for clan is Tł'ááshchí'í (Red Bottom). The daughter of Janette Nez and John Scott, she is the only one of her three brothers and two sisters to work silver.

Gene's dad was a silversmith, doing mostly traditional file-and-chisel work, and following the oldest Navajo silverworking techniques, drawing his own wire and hammering sheet from ingot. Most of his work was plain silver because, Gene says, it was hard to get

OPPOSITE PAGE, TOP LEFT: Works by Martha and Gene Jackson.
THIS PAGE: Works by Tommy Jackson.

turquoise in those days. He learned from his father surreptitiously: "You know how them old-timers were; if you were watching them work it could ruin what they were doing." Watching inspired a desire to try his own hand, so when his dad would go on a trip, Gene would use a piece of baling wire to pick open the lock on his tool box. "Then my dad would get mad and ask who had been foolin' around with his tools. I'd say, 'Not me.'" As a young man, Gene went into the Army; when he came out, he attended Navajo Community College to "re-learn" silversmithing. He remembers Kenneth Begay as an instructor there then, but Begay did not teach him. "He didn't teach *any* of the men—he left that to his assistants. He preferred to teach the women," he notes wryly.

Martha, born north of Winslow, learned silversmithing from Gene, after they were married. It was silversmithing that helped her through the financial burden of earning her master's degree in education from the University of Arizona in 1981. She has been deeply involved in and committed to education her entire life. She teaches the Navajo language—

Tommy Jackson.

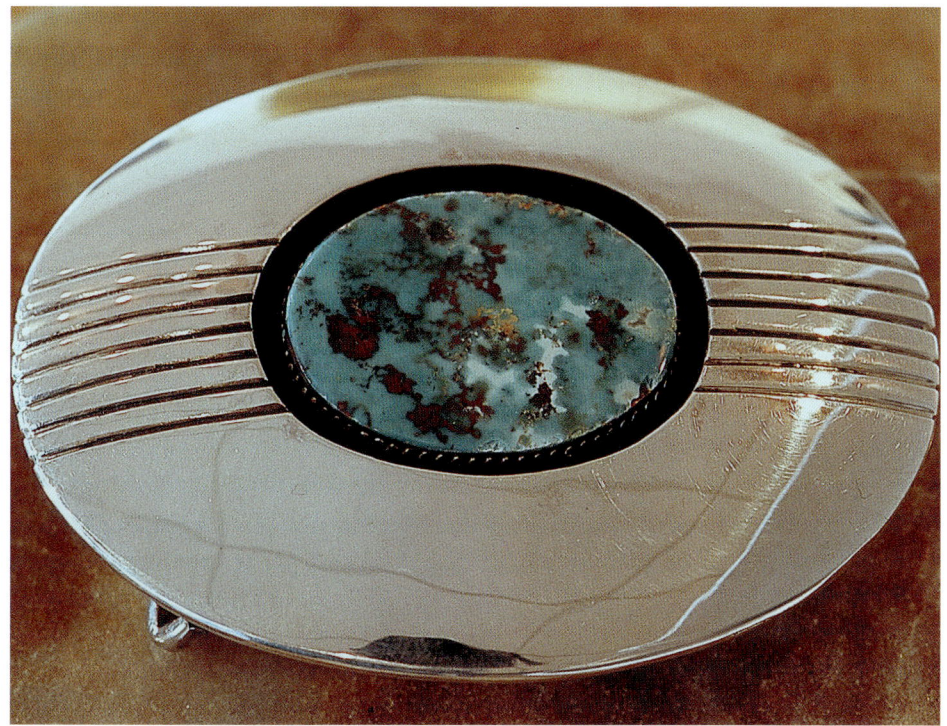

Shadowbox buckle by Martha and Gene Jackson

speaking, reading, and creative writing—and instructs other teachers in Navajo-language teaching methods. As she begins the eighth decade of her life, her dedication is still unwavering and she has yet to retire from the educational field.

Of their five children, youngest son Danny works as a substitute teacher (in addition to making jewelry); another has a degree in elementary education, and their daughter is completing her doctorate in education. Of the two other sons, one is a jack-of-all-trades and the other is an EPA enforcement agent.

Martha and Gene are best known for hollowware and shadow-box styles. The bracelet surface is decorated with stampwork motifs or carefully chiseled lines, accenting the range of stones, from top quality Morenci, Blue Gem, Chinese, Royston, and Sleeping Beauty turquoise to lapis lazuli, coral, Wild Horse alabaster, carnelian, and even meteorite. On occasion they even set the stone on the inside of a bracelet, a style some call "hidden beauty." This is a design innovation pioneered by the late Charles Loloma, a Hopi silversmith who was one of the great jewelry artists of the twentieth century. Gene does much of the shaping, but the hammering it requires is taking a painful toll on the joints of his hands. Yet while the quantity of work has slowed, the quality and pride of workmanship remain absolutely undiminished.

The son who makes jewelry full-time is their eldest: Tommy Jackson, born in 1958. He learned, not surprisingly, from his parents. "I started when I was about twenty," he says. "It was before I started teaching at Tohatchi. So, gosh, I've been silversmithing almost all my

Tommy Jackson.

Gene and Martha Jackson.

BELOW & OPPOSITE PAGE:
Works by Tommy Jackson.

life." He earned a degree in elementary education at the University of Arizona and afterward went with his wife, Marie, to teach at a school in Wide Ruins, Arizona. From there he went to Tohatchi, where he taught a silversmithing class. After several years of teaching he went full-time into jewelry-making. "I started with Gary Gordon at his place, BG Mudd in Gallup, where I picked up inlay," he recalls. "That was about 1985–86. I worked in both silver and gold and learned a lot from watching Benson Manygoats and Wilbert Muskett. After that I went in more for the old style—hammer, file, chisel, and stampwork. There was a lot of call for old-style concha belts around 2000 after Ralph Lauren's ads came out featuring them."

Taking a cue from his parents, Tommy is careful in his selection of stones, favoring the very best turquoise and coral he can find. His inlay work relies upon an even greater spectrum of materials, including ivory, shell, sugilite, charoite, malachite, alabaster, lapis lazuli, and jet.

He and Marie have seven children, several of whom are jewelers in their own right. "My stepson Nate [Blackrock] beat me at Santa Fe Market one year. Tommy Jr. is a roper, not a silversmith—but a great painter, though. And Nate just won the Indian National Rodeo Finals in San Carlos [Apache Reservation] in team roping. He tried for five years, missing once by 2/100 of a second, but then he got it," Tommy smiles. "His son—my grandson Jake—and my son Tommy Jr. roped together to win in junior rodeo."

Back in his workshop, where sons Owen (b. 1978) and Loren (b. 1984) can sometimes be found doing inlay work and buffing, respectively, Tommy leans back in a chair with a small Navajo weaving hanging on the wall behind him—a weaving he commissioned with the Harley Davidson logo on it. It matches a basket made for him by the famed Navajo basket-weaver Sally Black, also with the Harley logo, reflecting yet another interest of this on-the-go artist who can see the generations of silversmiths and educators in the family stretching as far back in the past as they do into the future.

CARLTON AND JULIE JAMON AND FAMILY
ZUNI

BORN IN 1962 IN ZUNI to Ben and Cornelia (formerly Cornelia Epaloose) Jamon, Carlton has one brother and three sisters. The sisters, Diana, Shelly, and Brenda, all do jewelry, and brother Benjamin also works silver. It runs in the family; Carlton's folks were also jewelers, known in particular for a style of earring and link bracelet where each link comprises a single elongated oval turquoise surrounded by half-round wire set on edge.

For a time Carlton stayed with—and learned from—his grandmother Winnie Jamon. The apprenticeship began when he was fourteen with filing and buffing, the laborious, onerous tasks that spell the difference between a fine piece of jewelry and a waste of effort. His first work was a ring, a no-frills affair made with a simple half-round wire shank set with a single turquoise in a plain bezel. His first silversmithing tools arrived unexpectedly, while he was working for his grandmother. "I had been buffing her cluster jewelry for her," he recalls. "It was an order of one hundred rings from Turney's shop in Gallup. I was thinking about all this money I would go home with when I got paid for my part of the work, but I went home with a box of tools she made me buy instead," he laughs.

"After I graduated from Zuni High School, I went to the University of New Mexico extension campus in Gallup for automotive mechanics, earning an associate of science degree about 1979.

"I started making jewelry on my own about the time I married Julie, in 1985. We were living in Fort Defiance, and I didn't have a job or anything, but my wife's coworkers at the

OPPOSITE PAGE, TOP RIGHT:
Work of Alex Jamon.

Julie, Carlton, and Alex Jamon.

hospital found out I was Zuni and wanted jewelry all the time, so I started making simple inlay kinds of things and selling to them."

A couple of years after that they moved to Albuquerque, where Julie earned a degree in health education at UNM. A cousin of Carlton's was making jewelry. "He was down and out, battling some personal problems, but really talented," says Carlton. "I learned how to do a lot of different kinds of repairs from watching him. He did needlepoint work and a lot of contemporary stuff, but he never got paid that well for doing it. He could go through his scrap drawer and make something really neat. I wanted to help him out, help him straighten out his life, so we planned to make jewelry together. We went out and bought all the tools he said we needed. But after a little while, I ended up being the only one doing it." Three years later, in 1989, their second son, Alex, was born and they moved back to Zuni.

Julie and Carlton collaborate on the hollow silver bear pendants that give their business, Silver Bear, its name, but each produces individual work as well. They have a shop in Zuni and formerly ran one in Gallup. A website—www.silverbearstudio.com—was begun at the same time. "It started out because I always wanted one [a website] but didn't have a clue what it was, but knew I wanted one," Carlton laughs. "I finally traded a guy in Phoenix $1,000 in jewelry in return for building the website. We were proud of it but there was no Internet connection in Zuni, so I couldn't show anyone. Finally I got it on a CD to show people. Then my oldest son, Jeffry, got interested in it. He couldn't believe how much I paid for it, so he really got into it and made a website for me. Then he started his own business building websites—in the eleventh grade! He named his business Dynamic Accretion. He does graphic art. At the Santa Fe Indian Market he had huge pieces, three feet by four feet, on paper, sandwiched in between Plexiglas—narratives with graphics."

About the time Carlton and Julie decided to close their Gallup store in favor of their Zuni studio, Catholic Charities approached them about running a shop in its building on the old Route 66 in Gallup. The Jamons currently operate the business, Native Hands co-op, at the Catholic Charities of Gallup's Indian Center. Carlton is also one of the founders of the Zuni Cultural Arts Council (ZCAC), which promotes local artists and teaches them how to sell directly to the public.

The idea for the ZCAC came from a bad show at Casa Grande's O'odham Tash. "It was cold, windy … just terrible," Carlton recalls. "All the artists were showing outside the tent, and they were freezing. All the dealers and the people who were buying were inside the tent. The artists made a petition to correct this situation but it didn't make a difference. Nothing did. On the way home Julie and I were thinking that it was really unfortunate we had to deal with this. This shouldn't happen. We decided to have a show at home to show others how it should be done: treating artists with respect." It took some time, public meetings, and a decision to create an organization by, of, and for the artists. It happened with financial support from the tribe and donations from businesses in Zuni. It provided a retail market once a year for Zuni artists and, even more important, workshops where artists could learn how to better price and market their work and how to work more smoothly and fairly with the traders and dealers. "It is about a lot of encouragement and just about being more professional and not afraid to try new things," he says.

Youngest son Alex is creating his own jewelry. "When we moved back to Zuni," says Carlton, "my sister gave us her garage to set up a studio in there. Alex grew up in there watching me work. One day he said, 'I need 18-gauge plate and 14-gauge round wire and I want to make this'—and he had a drawing of a necklace. He was about eleven then. We went to a show at the Museum of Northern Arizona in Flagstaff, and he entered it and got the Young Artist award [in 1999]." Dad helped him only with finishing tips; it was all Alex's work.

Alex describes making that first piece: "I drew it out and then basically my dad told me the basics. That is pretty much the way I work: think about it a lot then put it onto paper, then make it." Asked about what he draws upon for inspiration and ideas, he replies simply, "Contemporary life."

AL JOE
NAVAJO

THE OLDEST OF FIVE BROTHERS AND THREE SISTERS, Al Joe was born in Winslow, Arizona, in 1950 to Robert Joe of Burnt Corn (near Piñon, Arizona) and Rosanne Joe (formerly Rosanne Begay) of Dilkon, Arizona. Neither of his parents worked silver; they were ranchers. Al learned silversmithing from an uncle, Colbert Joe Sr., who was not only an accomplished smith but had opened his own shop in Fort Defiance, Arizona, employing several smiths in the early 1970s.

After graduating from Winslow High School in 1970, Al says, "I was going to college at Flagstaff and I wanted some money, so I'd drive *all* the way over there every weekend and he taught me the basics. I had taken a class at NAU (Northern Arizona University), but it was real different from what my uncle was doing. He started me out on sawing, then soldering. Soldering was the hardest thing to master in the beginning.

"One weekend I had managed to make a bracelet and a watch bracelet. Singer-style chip inlay. I was going back on Sunday, and my uncle told me where I could sell it: 'Last gas station on your right!' The following week I used the money and bought more silver."

Eventually, aided by his improving skills and the boom period in Indian art, he opened a silver workshop in Winslow called Little Squash. "I was still learning, but people were buying left and right, and I knew how to market it." At its peak he employed about twenty-five silversmiths, with some doing piecework at home and some working in the shop.

His brother Larry is a full-time engineer, having graduated from NAU in 1987 with a degree in civil engineering. He currently works for the Fort McDowell Apache Tribe and finds a little time to silversmith. "It's one of my hobbies," he says. "I picked it up from Al when I was just getting out of high school." Their sister, Rita Cordalis (b. 1954), works silver when she can take time from her duties as the art gallery curator at Fort Lewis College in Durango, Colorado. (She earned a degree in museum studies from the University of Colorado, Boulder.) Her style is distinct from that of her brothers, beginning with the stones that she sculpts and sets. The sculpted stone, usually fossilized ivory, jet, or ebony, is

generally accented with a piece of coral or natural turquoise. She picked up silversmithing from Larry, also while in high school. She says, "Al was busy at his workshop in town but Larry had a small workbench at home where I had the opportunity to not only watch him work but to try it myself."

For Al, things changed dramatically in 1980 when he borrowed Larry's "murdercycle." He was hit by a drunk driver and badly injured, with two severely broken wrists. His right hand still has circulatory problems and numbness, which forced him to give up bronc and bull riding. (He switched to team roping, an event his oldest son also participated in while in high school.)

About that time, well-known jeweler Gibson Nez offered some blunt advice: "You're good. Why don't you try to make a few pieces of good jewelry instead of just production work?" Al took his advice and went back to NAU, where he studied jewelry under Joe Coronet, learning many of the techniques Al has become famous for, including anticlastic raising.

He started working in gold a little in the 1980s. "Then, I would say about '97, I had a guy, Paul Dumont, from New York who had a gallery there, called Kokopelli. He liked my work and wanted some of it in gold and wanted to do a show to showcase my gold work. That was in June. He helped me get started by helping me get the gold. On the way to New York I did the Eiteljorg show [in Indiana], got two orders on pieces already sold. I reinvested all that. Otherwise I would never have been able to get into gold."

About the same time he started his signature low-dome shadowbox style with the specially curved outer edge. On a couple of occasions traders have offered to hire him to teach their silversmiths his techniques and style of work. Al offers to do so—for a salary, royalties on his designs, and a fifteen-year contract. The market does not always understand the level of dedication, innovation, and practice that goes into developing a unique style like Al's. But even when the day comes that others begin to copy his style of work extensively he is prepared: he has other techniques and styles in reserve.

Al also has found time to give back to his community. From 1991 to 1995 he served a term as tribal councilman from the Dilkon Chapter. But politics was not for him. "Well, one thing I found out was, in politics you can't satisfy everybody," he says. "In art I can satisfy all my customers. And I get a more happy feeling, feel more content with that."

Though he retreats to his workshop near Dilkon to work silver, Al and his wife, Fern (an administrative nurse for the Indian Health Service), live in Albuquerque. All of their five children are following other career paths, but a niece, Marcella (b. 1996), is learning silverwork from him. Still young, she has a way to go, but she is getting an early start from one of the best silversmiths she could hope to learn from.

FRANCES AND GEORGE JONES
NAVAJO

"NOBODY HAS EVER COME FORWARD to ask me these questions," says Frances Jones during an interview for this book. "I just do the work and sell it. They probably don't know who Frances Jones is."

This Navajo sand-cast-jewelry artist was born in 1943 at Fort Wingate, New Mexico. Her father, Fred Begay, was a hardworking, versatile silversmith from Manuelito Canyon, east of Gallup. Manuelito Canyon was home to a large number of silversmiths, many of whom, like her father, worked for the late Dean Kirk. He had a small store on the old Route 66 not far from Manuelito, where Fred and his father (also a silversmith) were born. Fred Begay never signed his work, which was extensive and varied: overlay work, hammered work, sand-casting, squash-blossom necklaces, pillboxes, and large boxes. He tried to teach his daughter how to make those boxes, but Frances was not interested in that type of work. "I started out with sand-casting jewelry when I was fourteen or fifteen," she says. "When I was real young I used to just help my dad do his work."

She too worked for Kirk, as well as selling to many of the other big names in the Indian arts business after World War II, including Tobe Turpen Sr. and Jr., Marion Woodard, Tom Woodard, John Kennedy Sr., the Navajo Arts and Crafts Guild, Fannie Etsitty, and Katie Noe. Now, she says, she sells "mostly just to Fannie [Etsitty], Ron Benally, and some *Bilagaanas* [Anglos] in Albuquerque."

After a lifetime of work, she modestly observes, "It didn't get me rich, but it kept food on the table."

If you have never taken a piece of sand-cast jewelry from the just-cast rough stage to the final polish, you have no idea how demanding, time-consuming, and dirty the task is. Frances knows. And consequently she prefers to sell her work rough and "let them do the dirty work," figuring that the slightly lower price she receives is worth it.

"I just sell to those peoples and after that I never know what they do with it. My granddaughter, she goes to UNM in Albuquerque. She asked me how I sell my jewelry. I just make this jewelry for people so they can sell them again. She said, 'Do you know that these people make a lot of money from your work? You can do better by selling directly to the customers. I'm going to try and help you. I'm going to sell it on a website.'" But for Frances, the higher price she would receive has its drawbacks, including selling one or two items at a time instead of a batch all at once, waiting for buyers, increased opportunities for others to copy her work (already a problem of long standing), and, most significantly, having to buff and polish. It is a possibility that will have to wait for the next generation. That's her son George, who already has taken over much of the work, though he still signs her hallmark to her designs because "they are her work, not mine. She's the one who came up with those designs and made them for so long. I'll use my hallmark on designs I come up with." Explains his mother, "Most of the figures I did myself—others came down from my dad. My dad had them. He carved them out. We got them from him." Only a few designs came from orders from or collaborations with people for whom she made jewelry.

Hardworking and frugal, they work with scrap silver, not with casting grain purchased from a supply house, to save money. Despite that, Frances has refused offers to mass-produce her work with her name on it in exchange for royalties. She objected because of the possibility that buyers might not be told that it was machine-made. She signs her work "FJ," a hallmark she has used since 1970. "Sometimes I still forget to sign," she admits. But it is her dedication and her integrity, now passing into the next generation, that truly mark the work.

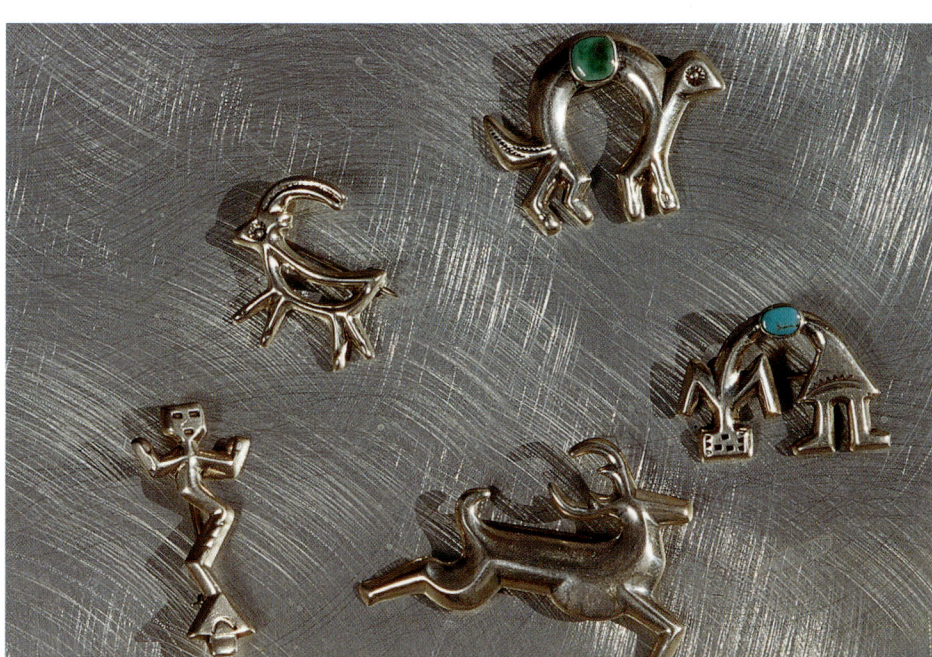

DOROTHY POLEYMA AND RAYMOND KYASYOUSIE
HOPI

HUSBAND AND WIFE SILVERSMITHS RAYMOND AND DOROTHY each bring a different approach to work, and each has traveled a different path to a career as a silversmith artist.

Raymond found his calling early on. One of three sons and three daughters, he was born in 1957 to Ranspie and Elina (Nutumya) Kyasyousie. A 1975 graduate of the Phoenix Indian School, he and older brother Tony apprenticed at Hopicrafts, an operation run by two brothers—Emory and the late Wayne Sekaquaptewa. (Emory was the first Hopi to earn a law degree, and he spearheaded the arduous and important task of creating the first Hopi dictionary.) Like many smiths who learned their craft at the Hopi Guild in that era, Raymond was instructed by the highly talented and well-regarded Hopi silversmith Glenn Lucas. Glenn taught less by direct instruction than by watching the men work and advising them as they proceeded. Practicing in less expensive copper and brass first, they graduated to silver after a month or so. "I started off with earrings and pendants," says Raymond. "Pendants are easier to do—they don't have to match up," he grins.

Over the years he has worked for several other Indian arts businesses. He lasted only a week at a sweatshop operation in Gallup, explaining that "there were too many folks." He moved to the Phoenix area to work for jewelry wholesaler Phil Tenneholz in Scottsdale, working at the Tenneholz home for a while, along with fellow Hopis Steven Sockyma, who was the foreman, and Elgen Sehongva. After several years there he moved on to the Trails End Shop, where another very talented and innovative Hopi artist, Roy Talaheftewa, worked. In 1984 he returned home to Hopi to work for the late Phil Sekaquaptewa and has been working for Von Monongye's shop on Third Mesa, just outside Old Orayvi (formerly spelled Oraibi) village, since 1987.

But he was not alone on that journey. Raymond, a member of the Greasewood Clan, met Dorothy, a member of the Badger Clan, in 1976 when he was nineteen and she was sixteen; they have been together since. While in Phoenix, Dorothy, born in 1960 to Ramona Loloma and Walter Poleyma, earned an associate's degree in business administration at Lamson in 1980. Her career path included a year-and-a-half stint at the National Institute of Health in Phoenix, the Hotevilla Community Center, and the tribal council, and as an administrative aide for then-vice-chair Vernon Masayesva, continuing into his chairmanship. They had returned home from Phoenix for the birth of their son Adam (currently studying fine art at Phoenix College) and then, pregnant with their second son, Willard, she began thinking of a new career, one that she could do at home.

Dorothy and sisters Sandra and Christine were nieces of famed Hopi artist Charles Loloma. "Ta'ah [Uncle] would let us, his nieces, use some of his tools," she recalls. "We learned how to solder, and we were introduced to sand-casting, lost-wax casting, and stonecutting and grinding. The first piece I made was a peace symbol, but he wanted us to do abstract and made us melt it down. But there were so many of us that it was hard on his patience. Verma [Verma Nequatewa, another of Loloma's nieces, who was also his apprentice] really helped.

"I started out in 1992 making stampwork bangle bracelets, and then I learned how to set stones and sold them at Monongye Gallery. Mostly I was making swirls … basic designs, but I had requests to do figurative designs. From that, clan symbols were added, and from there I began incorporating clan stories into my work. Ta'ah said there is beauty in nature, that what is important is the feeling as well as the presentation, and that I should look around nature and our surroundings." While she admits she did not fully grasp his advice as a young girl, its meaning has emerged for her now.

Katsina figures are something of a specialty of Raymond's, with a particular focus on Hopi koshares (clowns) goofing off. Dorothy is currently experimenting with textured sheet silver (replacing an earlier method she used, fusing silver filings on sheet silver to create texture). She also creates "abstract modern jewelry where I incorporate amethyst, garnet, and agate as well as turquoise, coral, and malachite. I like working with a multitude of stones, as they have healing properties."

Though their work is different, the words Dorothy speaks apply to the artists equally: "Ta'ah said everyone has talent, a gift. Beauty touches everyone and flows through everyone."

LARANCE–DENIPAH FAMILY
HOPI/ASSINIBOINE (STEVE) AND
NAVAJO/SAN JUAN PUEBLO (MARIAN)

STEVE WIKVIYA LARANCE AND HIS WIFE, Marian Denipah, are nothing if not energetic. In fact the whole family seems to be in constant motion. Family members are each pursuing their individual areas of interest in venues across the Southwest and doing it with the support of the rest of the family, who frequently drop what they are doing to help one another. Catching up with them took some doing—nearly a year, in fact.

Steve was born in 1958 to Rosella Albert (Hopi) and Ed Lawrence (Americanized from the original French, LaRance, and Steve has since changed it back), an Assiniboine from Fort Belknap, Montana. Rosella and Ed had met while attending boarding school at Haskell Institute in Kansas. Many years later, their grandson Nakotah would play the film role of an Indian student at that same boarding school.

A member of the Sun Clan at Upper Munqapi Village, Steve spent part of his childhood with grandparents Steve and Zelma Albert, starting high school in nearby Tuba City. "In high school, maybe about 1974, I took a jewelry class," he recalls. "I remember the first thing I made was a bowguard. I wore it in a dance at Hopi. But I didn't continue with it." He finished high school at Coconino High in Flagstaff and went on to pursue an accounting degree at Northern Arizona University, while teaching three-dimensional art and design at Coconino Community College. The NAU Indian Club sponsored a powwow that drew students over from the Institute of American Indian Art in Santa Fe. Says Steve, "I never knew about [IAIA]. I might have gone there if I had known about it."

One of those students was Marian Denipah, born in 1959 at San Xavier, just outside Tucson on the Tohono O'odham Reservation. Her parents, Gordon Denipah and Natalie Cata, both worked in public health. Consequently Marian grew up across the Southwest: Shiprock, Taos, Window Rock, San Xavier—wherever there was an Indian Health Service hospital or clinic. She is an enrolled member of the Navajo Nation (as is their oldest daughter, Nizhoni), but she retains close ties to her mother's pueblo of San Juan, and the family frequently returns there for feast days as well as other religious observances and family occasions. Her high school years were spent in Tucson, where she was influenced by her art teacher. "Mr. Palmer was a fantastic portrait artist and I decided that I wanted to be one, too," she says.

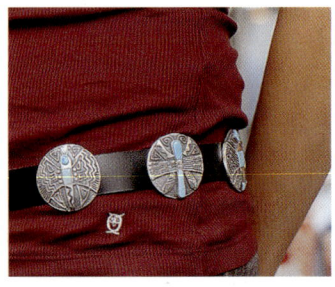

At her mother's urging, Marian earned a certificate from IAIA in 1983 before moving to Flagstaff and earning a BFA in art from NAU in 1997. "It was through Marian that I reconnected with art," Steve says. "I went with her to shows and thought, 'I should be doing something.' I had carved katsinas when I was younger, but I didn't want to compete with all the other katsina carvers. Marian is the one who suggested stone sculpture." In short order his work, in limestone and alabaster, won top prize in sculpture at the Museum of Northern Arizona's Hopi Show and in 2001 at the Arizona State Museum's Southwest Indian Arts Fair. "I want to do bronzes," he says. "I'm way past due trying that. I hope to do that in the next couple years—but I've been saying that for some years," he grins.

Marian began in two-dimensional art and, in addition to jewelry, continues to create mixed-media works in her studio, where her children all spent time growing up and learning to paint under the patient encouragement of their mom. Diligence as well as patience are important parts of Marian's approach to art. While studying art she naturally took anatomy, but she wanted to do more than simply pass another class, she says, so "I took anatomy four times because I really wanted to 'get it.'"

It was not until after son Nakotah was born in 1989 that Steve began to work silver. Says Steve, "We had a studio and arranged to share the space with the Navajo jeweler Ric Charlie in exchange for his sharing his knowledge of sand-casting." Charlie is widely renowned for his unique approach to sand-casting. This silverworking technique, frequently set with stones, is what the LaRance-Denipah family has become well known for.

Nizhoni (b. 1982), now a mother herself, began following her mother into the studio while still a toddler, and it was natural for her to follow her into jewelry as well, though she is also working toward her master's degree in physiology at the University of Arizona.

"We tried to impress on our kids that art is not just visual arts; it includes the performing arts," says Marian. This is a lesson that Nakotah, in particular, has embraced. Steve's sister (Lynnae Lawrence) is a shawl dancer and, says Steve, "When Nakotah was four my sister took him on the powwow trail with her. He got to see all that Plains Indian-style dancing and even met world-champion hoop dancer Derrick Suwaima Davis. He got inspired and started as a fancy dancer. We supported and encouraged him. He has been national champion in his age category for six years. He has also had roles in five movies. His big role was as Voices-That-Carry in the movie *Into the West*. Most recently he was in *Expiration Date*, a really interesting indie production by Rick Stevenson." And like many kids his age, he has also gotten interested in Japanese anime (animated cartoons).

Shondien (b. 1992) won recognition for her sand-cast silver jewelry at the MNA Hopi Show and Indian Market in Santa Fe in 2004, while she was still in middle school. Notes Steve, "She paints, too, like her mom. Like all the kids, she went to the studio when her mom was working and was given a little space in which to work and materials to use. Our son Cree (b. 1993) is into sports, from basketball to hoop dancing, but I want him to try sculpture as well. This year (2006) he won first in jewelry in the youth division of both the Hopi Show and the Navajo Show at the Museum of Northern Arizona. Growing into dance and theater has been interesting for our family, and I'm excited about the future," enthuses Steve. "It's really incredible how things have taken off for the family. We also try to stay involved in Hopi religious life; that is a big part of our life. That and San Juan. It brings us back in tune; it re-inspires and re-invigorates."

It is interesting to note that Marian's great-grandmother, Regina Cata, worked as a cook at IAIA while Marian was attending. Mrs. Cata, born in Spain and brought to New Mexico by her grandfather, married a man from San Juan Pueblo at age thirteen. She influenced doll-making and even pottery-making at the pueblo and wrote the book *Runaway Boy*, illustrated by Santa Clara artist Helen Hardin.

ALLISON LEE
NAVAJO

ONE OF EIGHT CHILDREN OF CHEE AND RENA LEE, Allison is the only one working silver. Born to the Bit'ahnii (Folding Arms) Clan and for the Tsi'naajinii (Black-Streaked Wood) Clan in 1958 in Mexican Springs, New Mexico, he started silversmithing when he was fourteen. "My mom and my uncle [Emerson Etsitty Sr.], who pretty much picked up the craft on their own, were making squash blossoms, and I started out by helping them file beads, and then later I started soldering the bead halves," he says. "We used to string the halves on baling wire between two sticks mounted on asbestos board. The bead halves were pre-soldered. That is, each half had a bit of solder melted on the rim. We would flux them, heat the silver, and solder them together, turning the beads with tweezers to make sure there were no gaps. We'd solder twenty to thirty plain beads at a time that way.

"When I was young, I always asked them how much they sold their jewelry for. Once I asked my mom, 'How much did you sell that squash blossom for?' Her answer was $200. [This was during the boom period of the early to mid-1970s.] Twenty years later Mom asked *me*, 'How much did you sell that squash blossom for?' When I told her $1,800, she almost fell over, saying, 'Oh, no, we were giving them away!'

"When I was at Tohatchi High School, that was where I learned a lot. I took silversmithing classes, which were offered as an elective—like shop. There were beginning and intermediate classes taught by a Navajo lady, Mrs. Watchman."

When he was a sophomore, his biology teacher, Mr. Turner, used to cut stones and give Allison silver and cut turquoise to take home. He'd work on them and bring the finished jewelry back a week or so later. The teacher in turn would take the jewelry to sell, and two weeks later he'd pay Allison and provide more materials. Allison made a range of jewelry: bolas, bracelets, buckles, pendants, earrings, and rings. "I got my first vehicle that way, when I was a junior in high school—a 1969 Chevy Impala. My mom was a single parent, so it [the jewelry-making] helped out. We all had to go find jobs to support the family—to buy groceries, shoes for my sisters, clothes." At the time, Allison made mostly stampwork-style jewelry set with turquoise, along with a little overlay work.

During the summers, starting after his sophomore year, "I used to work in Gallup, for places like Richardson's Trading Co., Thunderbird, and James Rogers Silversmiths. There were lots of smiths working there, and I learned a lot of new shortcuts and methods." Before the silverwork lessons started there were floors to be swept and jewelry to be buffed and polished, but "after a while they kind of figured out that I knew how to do certain things, and gave me certain things to make."

Allison graduated from high school in 1977, about the time the boom period in Indian jewelry was tapering off. "The market took a hit and silversmiths were being laid off. You couldn't sell jewelry anymore; people were taking stones out and scrapping their work." (Silver prices eventually rose so high, doubling in sixty days in the fall of 1979 and hitting $50 an ounce by January 1980, that you could make more money—or at least make money more easily—by scrapping the silver you'd bought a couple of months before than by selling or *trying* to sell finished work.)

A career in jewelry certainly seemed ill-advised. "They were training uranium miners in Church Rock, New Mexico, for jobs that we were told would last the life of the mine—

Wyatt and Allison Lee.

twenty-five years. I was working in the haulage drifts, huge tunnels twenty by twenty feet, drilling, blasting, mucking, bracing, laying track. It was cool in there—raining all the time due to the water seepage. We built an underground dam to hold the water that was pumped out." He worked underground for about four years before being laid off in 1981 with thirty days' notice—two decades short of the promised tenure. "I think it was for a good reason that I didn't stay there, though it was an interesting job."

Allison went back to Mexican Springs and to silverworking. "I was making my own stuff, regular work. Among other places, I sold to The Storyteller Shop in Santa Fe, run by Rachael Elizondo. She was the one who suggested I make animal and cactus pins." She also suggested that Allison go to work for her son, Robert Elizondo, who owned a watch company called Eclissi. So Allison moved to El Paso, Texas, in 1981 and started to work for Eclissi, designing jewelry. As a part of the job, Elizondo took him to trade shows where he learned a great deal about marketing and pricing.

Missing home, he returned to Mexican Springs in 1984 and resumed his jewelry work, focusing on his successful line of "critter pins": cats, cows, roadrunners, hummingbirds, cacti, snakes, coyotes, and one of a coyote chasing a rabbit called "Fast Food."

He started working in gold in 1986, first making a gold bead choker. The following year he entered Santa Fe Indian Market for the first time. That was also the year he moved to Albuquerque and met his future wife, Nadine, who had been going to school at Northern Arizona University but was transferring to the University of New Mexico.

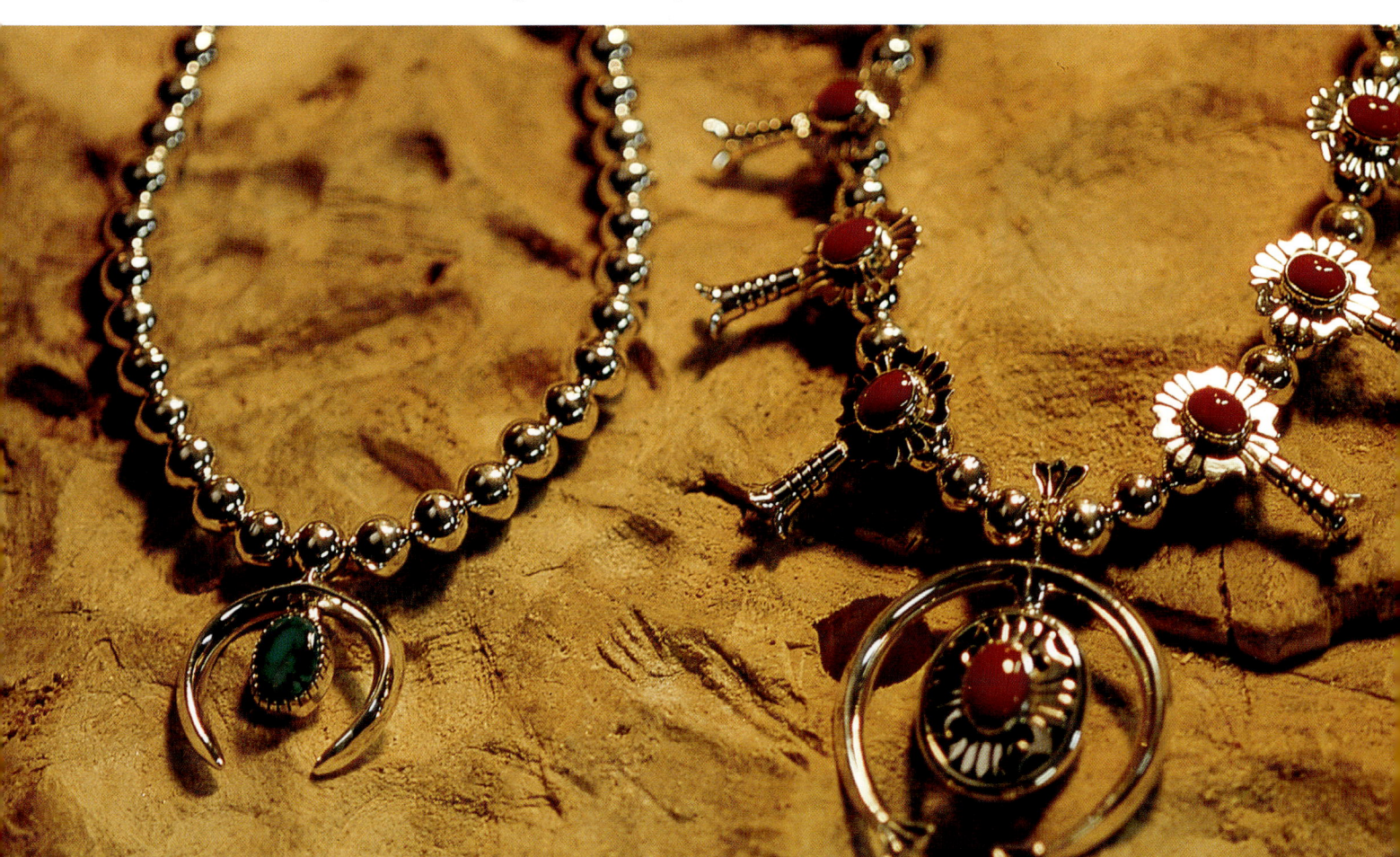

In 1988, with the help of Nadine, who has a degree in accounting, he incorporated and opened his own shop under the name Snowhawk, which he also used as a shopmark because "it got to where I couldn't keep up with orders, so I rented a shop in downtown Albuquerque and hired high school kids out of Cañoncito [now called Tohajiille, on the nearby Navajo Reservation] during the busy summer season." So successful were his designs that he had to travel to Tucson, Phoenix, Sedona, and Flagstaff every few weeks to sell to his museum and shop accounts.

In 1990 he decided to close the shop and focus exclusively on his own work. He continues to sell his work to a few shops, but focuses more on retail shows. "I have to do more retail since I work on my own … if you wholesale you have to hire other smiths to help." The cycle starts in February with a show at Litchfield Park, Arizona, and continues through the year, taking him from Arizona to New Mexico, Indiana, Oklahoma, Chicago, and Wisconsin.

At the shows he is able to network with other silversmiths, like Ray Tracey and Orville Tsinnie, who were especially helpful with advice early on. Orville, for example, would stop by his booth at shows to make helpful suggestions on pricing (including how to know if

86 SILVER & STONE

you are overpricing), marketing, and finishing tips. Other silversmiths whose work he admires are Vernon Haskie, Jake Livingston, and the late Herbert Taylor. Allison stays focused on the process, trying new techniques, different tools, constantly innovating and experimenting even as a bit of Mexican Springs stays with him: a cottonwood stump he brought from there in 1990 that he uses for his hammer work. "When I started it was much taller," he smiles.

Allison and Nadine have three sons: Wyatt, born in 1990, and twins Kyle and Trent, born in 1993. Wyatt began silversmithing at age thirteen. "He started kind of like I did: making beads," notes Allison. Wearing one of Apache artist Doug Miles's skateboard T-shirts, Wyatt says he started "because it was something to do, a way to earn some money, and I had been watching my dad do it for a long time." Asked what was the hardest thing to learn, he responds, "Probably soldering the beads together." Ironic, considering that it was a bead necklace for which he won a blue ribbon at the Santa Fe Indian Market in 2003 and yet another bead necklace that garnered the same award in 2004.

Allison's two oldest children have forged careers in other areas, with son Ferguson Lee working in the Douglas County (Colorado) County Clerk and Recorder's Office. Daughter Alvina Lee is a law school graduate of the University of Colorado and a practicing lawyer, also in Colorado.

CLARENCE AND RUSSELL LEE
NAVAJO

CLARENCE STARTED LIFE IN 1952 IN FORT DEFIANCE, ARIZONA, as one of six children born to Tom Lee and Emma Rose Lee. (Emma made the first Navajo Nation flag.) Clarence's great-grandfather, Jesús, was a Mexican sheepherder, kidnapped as a young boy and adopted by a Navajo family. All of Clarence's siblings work silver to one degree or another, with the exception of a sister who works in the health-care system.

His father was a remarkable man. He fought in the Pacific theater during World War II, survived the infamous Bataan Death March, and was a POW for four years; later, he was an entrepreneur and New Mexico's first Indian state senator. He was also a silversmith, of necessity. Owner of a trading post he'd started at Twin Lakes in eastern New Mexico, Tom Lee learned to make silver jewelry to supplement his income when business was slow. "I helped my dad when I was going to Tohatchi High School, selling his jewelry," says Clarence. "His style of silver was more or less traditional."

A Mrs. Hale was his first art teacher. Seeing the potential in his work, especially the jewelry that he sometimes sold to teachers, she admonished him, "Don't start giving stuff away." In school he made metal sculptures, and worked in oil and watercolor (and still does occasionally). He also pursued an interest in rodeo—calf-roping and team roping—attending rodeos in both Arizona and New Mexico. Clarence stopped shy of graduation as he had to help support his family. "I got married and had to get a real job. That was 1976."

His first silverwork was pretty traditional hammered and stampwork, set with stones. "I did that for maybe eight months. Then I kind of fell over backwards into that storyteller style. I made a bracelet first, then a pin. It was all plain silver at first. I didn't set any stones in it 'til later."

Clarence has always preferred to sell retail, at Indian art shows, competitions, and exhibitions. His first show was a free one at the Grand Canyon. After that he sought to sell his work at any place that was free as he struggled to make his name and make his expenses in the early days. (Booth fees currently run $300 or more, on top of travel expenses that can quickly drive show expenses for an artist up to $1,500 or more, as most artists customarily bring their families.) Those first shows provided the emerging silversmith encouragement; "I got a good response and it just opened up from there," he says. His first competitive show was the 1977 Navajo Fair, where his work garnered a first-place ribbon.

"I started signing, using an engraver at the beginning, using my family's registered brand stamp, Rocking Lee," he says. "Using the brand was my dad's idea originally. About 1988–89 I added my signature."

His son, Russell, was born in 1976. Clarence, a single dad, raised Russell alone since 1980, taking him along to the shows. "When Russell was about ten or twelve he wanted a toy he saw at the mall. I told him, 'You have to sell something first.' I guess that kind of encouraged him to try making silver." At times Russell's cousin Clinton would come along to the shows. Both now help Clarence full-time, and Clarence currently does twenty-five to thirty shows per year.

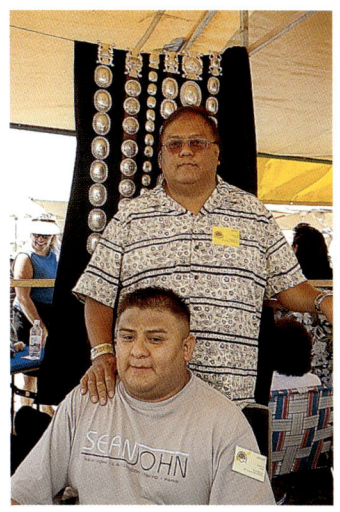

Clarence's father was raised by Claude Bowlin, who was in the crafts and souvenir business. Claude taught Tom a lesson that he in turn passed on to young Clarence: if you want to do well, you have to have plenty of inventory on hand. It has come at a cost, however; carpal tunnel syndrome has affected this industrious smith who can produce fifteen to twenty pins a day, while striving to maintain an inventory of a half-dozen or more each of the 300-plus different designs he has created (including a wind-up Christmas tree, a specialty piece he designed some years ago). Russell now does most of the cutting of the designs and does his own work as well, having acquired his own hallmark stamp about 1998. Clarence does all the stonecutting and has since about 1988. "I do the stampwork and everything else, then give it back to Russell to put on the findings and buff it," he says.

Many silversmiths have created or adapted equipment to facilitate their style of work or isolated circumstances. In Clarence's case it is the adaptation of IV bags for the water drip on his stonecutting and grinding equipment. Twice a year he takes all of his scrap silver and melts it down to use in a few special cast works that he creates.

Though he says he can see the result even before he finishes a new piece, the designs that Clarence is so famous for are usually sketched out first, sometimes while sitting in airports or during down time at hotels or even at his booth. At his booth he always attempts to keep the displays of his inventory interesting and fresh, trying new designs for four or five months. "If it doesn't go then we abandon it," he says. "But you never know. We used to make trucks (three-dimensional models) but sales slowed so much we stopped making them. Then as soon as we stopped, people started asking for them again. We make them in four different sizes. For the largest there are two dozen separate pieces of silver that we have to solder together to make that truck. The first truck we did for fun. We took it to the Gallup Ceremonial. It was something different, something to get some attention. I guess it worked because a lady from the British Museum came by and bought some work and interviewed me over three days. The truck pin with everybody in back is kind of our signature piece, as is the truck bracelet."

Among the silversmiths Clarence admires is Jake Livingston, whom he describes as "a nice guy who does nice work." Similar accolades can be accorded Clarence, who suffers from a mild case of dyslexia yet has built a successful career as a silversmith. And when he needs a break from silversmithing he can cross the yard to his welding shop, where he makes stands and cases and has built a barbecue grill with a smoker and a dumping trailer he designed. Then back to his silversmith bench.

JAKE LIVINGSTON
NAVAJO

THE DECISION ON WHO MIGHT BE INCLUDED in this volume was far and away the most difficult task I faced. One of the first silversmiths I interviewed was Allison Lee. In the course of the interview my other half, Emmi, thought to ask him who else's work he admired. Allison mentioned several names, including Jake Livingston. It was such a great question, I frequently asked it in subsequent interviews. When one silversmith after another mentioned Jake Livingston—the man and his work—I knew he had to be included.

Jake was born Jacob Haloo Jr. in 1946 to Jacob (Jake) Haloo Sr., of Zuni, and Lola Pinto, who is Navajo. Jake's tribal affiliation is Navajo, following the maternal line, but he is fluent in both Navajo and Zuni. (There was a time when it was not unusual for a member of a Southwest tribe to speak three or more languages.) He was born at Pinehaven, New Mexico, midway between Zuni and Gallup, but went to elementary school at Zuni and high school on the Navajo Reservation at Fort Wingate, finally graduating from Window Rock High School in 1966. All of his brothers and sisters make jewelry, beginning with brothers Wayne and Alvin and his sisters Lolita Natachu, Nancy Laconsello, and Rolanda Haloo.

After high school he joined the Marine Corps. He laconically describes that time: "I was in Vietnam '68–'69. Tripoli ship-helicoptered back and forth. Got back in fall of '69, wounded. Three Purple Hearts. Came back home, got trained as an operating engineer—heavy equipment. Trained in Phoenix." After the service, seeking a name for himself rather than being a junior, "I took a name from my uncle's side of the family": Livingston.

He had watched his father work and helped him out when he was younger. "My father, he's the one that taught others," he says. "I watched him, helped out. At the same time I did a little inlay: cardinals, eagles, bluejay, and hummingbird … different kinds of animals on special order." As he developed his skills he stepped up to greater challenges, including making a reversible necklace with thirty-two birds in gold. Not long after that Jake built a four-sided gold necklace. "A man wanted to trade a Rolls Royce for it. I didn't know what that was," he smiles.

The reversible pendants, sometimes called spinners, were the result of trying different types of work, including a four-sided pendant he made in 1972. He left heavy equipment during the boom period and went full-time into jewelry. "I met Gibson [Gibson Nez] and Andy Kirk when he started. And Ben Nighthorse—he encouraged me to do direct sales, said my work was too good to wholesale." Gibson, Andy, and Jake traveled to shows together to save money. "Sometimes one or the other makes the sale, or we travel all over and *don't* make the sale," he grins. Gibson tells the story of Jake feeling low from a cold and getting up in the middle of the night to drink some NyQuil, but winding up with a mouthful of blue dye. It took a month to completely get rid of the blue tongue and teeth. Years later, Gibson still laughs until the tears come in telling the story. Asked for confirmation of the story, Jake's face splits in a big smile.

A versatile silversmith who is conversant with both Zuni inlay and Navajo hammered and stampwork techniques as well as overlay, Jake first entered juried competition with "a reversible concha belt—all birds—nine conchas or so. Entered it into Gallup [Intertribal Ceremonial]. Got Best of Show. After that it took off." He entered and won ribbons at a series of shows including Santa Fe Indian Market, Red Earth, Heard Museum, Casa Grande's O'odham Tash, Eiteljorg Museum, and Eight Northern Pueblos. "Always needed something new each time. Usually set my work with Nevada Blue spiderweb I bought from Herb Bender out of California."

Jake's wife, Irene Owens, does the leaves and flowers in the inlay work that Jake creates. Those pieces are hallmarked "J&I LIVINGSTON." Jake started out with "JL" and since 1976 has used "JAKE L." Sons Jason (b. 1976) and Jay (b. 1979) have also helped out, which is how they learned. Like his father, Jay does both stamp and chisel work and some inlay, signing his work "JAY." Jason signs his work simply "J"; he began creating and selling his own items in the sixth grade. He entered Indian Market as a teenager and won first place. As his father notes, "He's still getting first place." Father and son Jason even attend shows and go on selling trips together.

Jake continues to experiment, and as he does, so continues the cycle so familiar to most jewelers of helping and being helped in turn. Jewelers Lyndon Tsosie and Kim Johnson gave him advice on how to work platinum for a special order that included a multistone inlay representing night and day, a band that included the moon, wolf, and stars for night, and sun, water, and mountains for day. An admirer of Jessie Monongye's work, he saw a piece he especially liked and thought he'd go ahead and make one like it himself. Jessie, with whom he attended Fort Wingate High School, gamely provided stone and advice for the project.

Jake's skills extend to other media. While in high school he learned how to carve leather and got interested enough to go to a school at Pinedale, Wyoming, for saddlemaking. "It's very time-consuming—more time than working with silver or gold—so I left it," he says. But not before building a silver-encrusted saddle. Similarly, he learned how to do bronze polychrome sculpture. "I just picked it up," he says modestly. But like the saddlework, though he keeps his hand in it, his focus is his jewelry. He observes with a smile in his eyes, "You can't jump on the plane with a bronze or a saddle."

GERALD LOMAVENTEMA
HOPI

LOMAVENTEMA (LIGHTNING) IS THE NAME GERALD WAS GIVEN during initiation into the Hopi Wuwutsim society. Born to Jerry and Mae Rose Honwytewa in 1967, he lost his mom when he was in elementary school, and was sent to Keams Canyon Boarding School and then to Sherman Indian High School. "That's where everybody went—there or Phoenix Indian School," he says. "Sherman was fun—a lot of people from different tribes. They had a jewelry class at Sherman, but I didn't take it. Same with ceramics, but I was more into sports—cross-country. I wasn't real good, but I was on the team. Our oldest daughter is on the Bruins [Hopi High School] cross-country team." He and wife Yvette Talaswaima have three daughters: Selene, Jerolyn, and Joanikka. In April of 2005, after twelve years of civil marriage, they were married in a traditional Hopi wedding ceremony—an event that stretches out over several days and involves family, clan relatives, and friends in a series of rituals and exchanges that create ties that bind everyone together.

After graduating from Sherman in 1985 he worked as a firefighter and went to trade school at Phoenix Tech in 1986; he specialized in facilities service, including basic wiring, plumbing, and general building maintenance. He was there for eight months but says, "I couldn't survive there. There were a lot of job opportunities, but I couldn't manage … there was the expense and I didn't have any relatives there neither, so I came back home. That is when they were offering training at Hopi Guild; my uncle told me I should go. I had seen it [silverwork] done when I was younger, but I didn't take any interest in it, but this time I

did. They started us on copper to practice. Not even a month later and I was already making silver jewelry for sale. I started with small earrings that are still my best sellers. The Guild would issue us silver, subtract the cost as the finished work came in, and pay us. One thing I used to make a lot of was bola tips," he smiles. There for nearly ten years, he started out on his own in 1997.

"I sometimes sold work outside the Hopi Cultural Center and one time [in 2001] I met a lady, Joan Caballero, who had been a judge at Indian Market. She encouraged me to go there to show my work. So I went to San Juan Pueblo's Feast Day, then to Santa Fe where I rented a space at the La Fonda Hotel for one day for $75. We were kind of out of the way; only people on the way to the restroom would find us," he laughs.

That same year he was approached by Roy Talahaftewa, who started the Putavi Project, also called Grandmother's Dream, to help Hopi silversmiths learn new techniques. "I thought, 'What the heck—I should try it out.'" Talahaftewa's project has had a major impact on the work of many Hopi jewelry artists.

"Steve LaRance came in [to Hopi] to do a workshop [in 2002] on sand-casting. As kids we carved molds and poured the lead from old car batteries, so I knew the basic idea. Besides tufa-casting I learned stonecutting from Roy, hollow-forming from Duane Maktima, and wax-carving from Phil Navasya, also stonecutting."

Gerald's wife also has a hand in jewelry-making. "I taught her how to work silver and she started making chain in 2004, and the first time we took the chains to the Heard Museum shop we sold them all out."

In creating his work he generally draws out the design first, frequently making a pattern of it from copper, and then carves the design into tuff for sand-casting, even to the extent of carving the bezels in which he sets the stones or inlay. His first sand-cast belt of katsina figures missed earning a prize at the Santa Fe Indian Market because regulations require that all sand-cast pieces be submitted with the tuff mold in which they were cast. Gerald's belt was composed of a dozen pieces, each cast in a separately carved mold, and he sent only a single, sample mold instead of the whole box.

He may have a learning curve ahead of him in negotiating the varied and sometimes contradictory rules for submissions to juried art shows, but his work proves he has mastered his chosen techniques and given full range to his imagination and vision.

MARY C. LOVATO AND FAMILY
SANTO DOMINGO PUEBLO

STONE AND SHELL WORK AT SANTO DOMINGO PUEBLO (where the people speak Keres and call their pueblo Kewa) is a Pueblo tradition that predates even this pueblo, which was founded about 1700. This story begins with Valentino Coriz, grandfather of Mary Coriz Lovato, who would take his work, leave the pueblo on foot on a trading expedition, and return months later sitting on a horse, driving a herd of sheep before him.

Valentino's son Santiago Leo Coriz (b. 1913) worked not only stone and shell, but also silver; he learned sand-casting from his childhood friend, Hopi silversmith Jimmie Kootswatewa. Jimmie's uncle, also a silversmith who did sand-cast work, buried the tuff he carved for his molds behind his little house. Young Jimmie and Leo dug some of it up and figured it out together. Leo was famous for his sand-cast work, and the tradition has continued in his family.

Mary was one of Leo's five children, all of whom learned to make jewelry. Mary started working in shell at age eighteen, instructed by her mother, Lupe Coriz. By the mid-1970s Mary was incorporating silver into her mosaics, using interesting and useful shapes of scraps left over from her husband's silverwork—a style she is still known for. Following a tradition that dates back to the early 1900s, she used to make thunderbird necklaces, but created them from new materials: plastic from Depression-era dishware, pieces of Edison records, and even pocket combs, mixed with turquoise and beads fashioned from gypsum from a mine in the nearby Sandia Mountains. (The turquoise the pueblo once used and

ABOVE & OPPOSITE PAGE: Work of Anthony Lovato, except for opposite page, top right: work of Mary Lovato.

BELOW & UPPER LEFT: *Anthony Lovato;*
UPPER RIGHT: *Mary Lovato.*

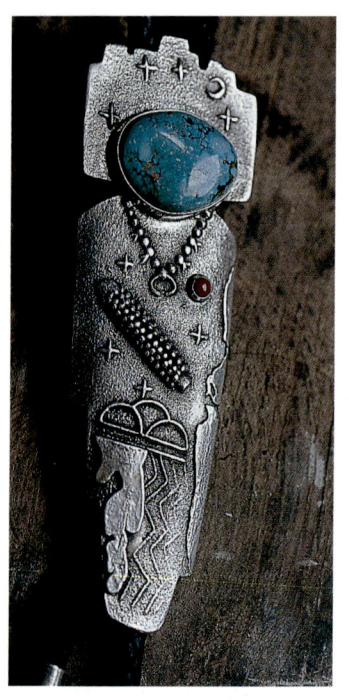

traded also came from nearby, the famed Cerrillos Mine.) This style died out in the decade after World War II, but on occasion it is still made on request.

Mary had six sons: Sedelio Jr., Harold, Anthony, Roderick, Nathan, and Isaac (Sedelio and Harold have both passed away). Both Harold and Anthony followed their grandfather's tradition of sand-cast work. Their grandfather told them where to find the tuff they used in their work, according to Anthony (b. 1958). "He told us, 'A Navajo family lives near where the tufa is.' We still take a loaf of bread or a watermelon to the old man who lives there when going to get tufa."

Nathan is doing fabricated work, inlay, and sand-cast with inlay. Nathan (b. 1967) started out learning from his mother by helping her as a teenager, grinding stone for mosaics and drilling shell for beads. On occasion he still makes shell-bead necklaces—"about one strand a month," he laughs. His interest in silverwork began when he watched his father and grandfather work, but it did not become his focus until after high school graduation and a stint in the US Army. "I got out in 1989 and then hitchhiked to California, where I lived for a year," he recalls. "Then I came back home in 1990, bought my tools, and started full-time. I use just the original tools: hammer, torch, stump, files … no fancy equipment. When I texture silver I take it out to the front step and hammer it in the concrete, kind of beat it up," he smiles. He cuts all his stones, from inlay to the cabochons in his earrings. He started out with a style he dubbed "Groovey Earrings"—traditional turquoise-slab earrings but with a groove carved around the edge to help hold a silver wire that attaches to the earring hook. It's a style that has since been widely copied, here and abroad. He still makes them, noting, "I sell to tourists and I sell to collectors." It is in the work he sells to collectors that his family's tradition is manifested. His mother's influence can be seen in the reversible earrings with a single stone on one side and a mosaic on the reverse. And the work and inspiration of both parents come into play with his inlaid sand-cast bracelets with stampwork designs on the inside.

Nathan has a daughter, Santana, born in late 2005, and a son, Danzel, who at age nine has begun to express an interest in jewelry-making. "I've got him started doing double-sided mosaic pendants," he says, proudly handing over a ready-to-grind-and-polish pendant set with black jet accented with a piece of red coral, with a turquoise slab on the reverse side.

Older brother Anthony's jewelry-making career began in 1975 when he started doing sand-cast work. "I learned from my dad and grandpa," he says. "Then I entered IAIA and got an associate's degree in fine arts in 1978. I tried a year at University of Colorado in Boulder and moved to Flagstaff in 1980 and worked at the Museum of Northern Arizona as an exhibit preparator and took jewelry classes at NAU until 1981." He moved to Keams

ABOVE: Mary Lovato;
BELOW: Anthony Lovato.

Work of Mary Lovato.

Mary and Anthony Lovato.

Canyon just before the birth of his oldest son, who is also the oldest great-grandson of famed Hopi potter Joy Navasie. Living there for two years, Anthony learned how to make Hopi-style pottery. "It taught me about positive and negative space and how to use that in my designing," he notes. Returning home, he left pottery-making behind. "Since 1984 I've been a full-time jeweler," he says. "I started out making a lot of jewelry—I had to get established—but then, as I got established and won recognition for my work, I've been able to slow down and spend more time on each piece." The work is demanding, and sand-casting can be as finicky as pottery-making. The week I interviewed Anthony had been one of those troublesome weeks: not a single satisfactory pour. But those rough patches—encountered by every jeweler—are by no means common. And his work is popular within the pueblo itself, as demonstrated by the fact that he was commissioned in 1993 to design and sand-cast sterling badges for the Santo Domingo Tribal Police Department.

Anthony's two older sons, Joel (b. 1984) and Cordell (b. 1988), are both learning to work silver, and both have already entered their work in competition and won ribbons. A proud father recounts, "They both got ribbons the same year, when they entered pieces at the Red Earth Show in Oklahoma. And they had started working silver on their own only two years before that." Now even Joel's little daughter, Allison, is learning jewelry-making, but focusing on her grandmother's style: mosaic work. It's a beginning. Or in the case of the Lovato family, another new beginning—with yet another on the horizon: Anthony's youngest son, Noah (b. 1990), has begun to express the curiosity that has launched so many jewelry artists.

Work of Mary Lovato.

RAY LOVATO SR.
SANTO DOMINGO PUEBLO

THE STORY OF THE JEWELRY OF RAY LOVATO is a story of family. Born in 1946 into a large family of eight sons and two daughters, he began by helping his mother, Tonita Reano, and father, Ike Lovato, in the late 1950s. "When I was ten or eleven years old, I helped drill turquoise with a pump drill, using carbide files for the drill points," he remembers. His mother "really liked it when I helped—I could drill faster than her! It took from two to five minutes to drill a hole through turquoise, depending upon hardness. I got to work inside while my brothers worked out in the field during the summer. My mom had a small grocery store in the house she sold things from. Mom kept giving me pop and stuff to keep me working," he grins.

Like many from the pueblo, his father traveled, trading his multicolor necklaces of jet, shell, coral, and turquoise as well as joclas, a particularly popular trade item. Every year, Ike visited a friend from his Albuquerque Indian School days in Fort Duchesne, Utah, bringing food they had harvested from their fields and trading Ike's jewelry along the way. Rather than traveling and trading extensively with other tribes, his father preferred to sell directly to a few dealers, often trading his work for rugs. Over the years Ike dealt with Hatch Trading Post in Waterflow, Monroe Foutz, John Kennedy Sr., Bob Leighton, and Roman Hubbell of Hubbell Trading Post in Ganado.

Ray found that learning was not so hard, "because my dad really knew what he was doing and taught me to do it the same way." A year after Ray started helping by drilling

stone and shell with a pump drill, he says, "my father bought his first electric drill, from Shipley's in Bayfield [New Mexico]. I use a Dayton drill now." Ray estimates that compared to a pump drill, an electric drill cuts the drilling time in half, depending upon the hardness of the stone. For grinding the shell and turquoise blanks down to a round shape, his father used a Briggs and Stratton motor to power a grinding wheel, a setup that Ray is planning on rebuilding or re-creating.

At age twenty Ray enlisted in the Army (1966–69), doing two tours of duty in Vietnam, one of them during the Tet Offensive. He left the service as a buck sergeant, his health impaired, but he remains "proud of what I did for our country."

After his return he went into construction. After being fired for the sixth time he decided to go back to doing what he had learned from his father: making jewelry. "Then I started to do what my father taught me, my own work. Then everything was okay—and I've never been fired since then," he laughs.

In 1974 he married Peggy Reano, and they now have seven children (three sons and four daughters), of whom four help him in his work. Ray is not just a jeweler, as he has fields that he farms during the summer, growing chiles, melons, corn, beans, and alfalfa, much as his father did—part of an ancient tradition of Pueblo farming that has produced crops uniquely suited to each pueblo's eco-region and water resources.

Like his father, Ray acquires turquoise from a variety of mines, primarily from traders who come to the pueblo to sell rough turquoise, both natural and stabilized. Natural turquoise cannot be slabbed easily like stabilized or treated turquoise, which is hardened

Lovato family booth at Santa Fe Indian Market, 2005.

with resin. Fracture lines in the natural turquoise (mined by blasting) can cause the turquoise to break or even crumble. "Sometimes it has fractures and breaks when you are drilling or even polishing it, and that makes you mad," he says. "When you first start using natural you can lose up to half, but as you get better it is more like a quarter, unless the stone turns out to be very brittle or fractured." With treated stone ranging between $50 and $200 per pound and natural turquoise running between $200 and $600 per pound, even a 25 percent loss with natural turquoise is a costly one. "You have to know what you are doing or you can really waste natural turquoise," he points out.

Not surprisingly, most beadworkers at Santo Domingo use treated turquoise. Ray is one of the few artists who frequently work with natural turquoise: "I like to challenge myself. After buying turquoise I have to think what I can do with it. The material tells you what it can be." Over the years he has used a range of turquoise, including Lone Mountain, Kingman, Orville Jack, Royston, and Sleeping Beauty, preferring turquoise that comes as small nuggets and does not require sawing. Instead, each piece is ground flat by hand and then drilled before being rounded and polished.

His daughters, notably Missy, help him with his work, but it is his son Andrew who is most seriously following in his father's footsteps, having won ribbons in the youth division at Santa Fe's Indian Market and now as an adult.

Ray enjoys working with beautiful turquoise, and his work has garnered many blue ribbons, but the awards no longer bring satisfaction. "A lot of judges anymore don't seem to know much," he complains. His work is worn happily and with pride by women and men across the country and in Asia and Europe, and it can be seen worn by dancers at the pueblo during religious observances. "That's good," says Ray, with satisfaction.

RICK MANUEL
GILA RIVER PIMA/TOHONO O'ODHAM

BORN IN SACATON, ARIZONA, IN 1950, famed Tohono O'odham jewelry artist Rick Manuel is registered with the Gila River Pima through his mom, Germaine Juan, even though he grew up on the Tohono O'odham reservation in his father Cipriano Manuel's village of Santa Rosa and is usually identified as Tohono O'odham. He is the oldest among his four sisters and two brothers, who are all enrolled with the Tohono O'odham Nation.

Like a lot of kids his age in the 1960s he was drawn to music, forming a rock-and-roll combo called the Renegades, which played at gatherings across the eastern half of the sprawling 2.8 million-acre Tohono O'odham Reservation and still occasionally gets together for a local gig.

A self-taught silversmith, he began experimenting with overlay work in 1976, having honed his cutting skills by sawing out the bison or the Indian on Indian-head nickels (minted between 1913 and 1938) and turning them into jewelry pendants. His first overlay pieces used desert scenes from the area around his village, establishing a unique style of overlay that is the hallmark of his work.

With his first wife, Norma Antone, a master horsehair-basket weaver, he has two sons. Growing up, both were helpers at one time or another, assisting with buffing and cutting, or being a general "gofer." Each, however, has chosen a different career path.

Rick moved into Tucson nearly twenty-five years ago, but he has traveled widely and spent extended time away, at such places as Monterey, Los Angeles, and Banning, California, where he worked as a carpenter as well as a silversmith. For many years he and his family would pick up in the summer and travel, selling the jewelry they had made until it was all gone, at which point they turned around and drove back to Tucson. Sometimes they got as far north as Pryor, Montana, where they attended Crow Fair. Another time it was the Feast of St. Geronimo at Taos Pueblo. Once it was New York City. "I always took my tools with me to build jewelry along the way," Rick says. "Once I made enough money to get to Boston. We stayed with some friends there while I built more jewelry. Then we stopped in New York and I sold $2,500 worth of jewelry in one shot, to the Museum of the American Indian. I thought 'wow,' and we thought we'd get an apartment and live there for a while, selling jewelry. Then we found it would take more than $2,000 just to move into a place. So we thought, 'Well, it's October, time to go home anyway,'" he laughs. "So we drove home, the five of us—my two sons, a brother-in-law, and my wife—in our old Camaro towing a U-Haul."

Rick's work draws upon the land, people, and traditions of the Tohono O'odham. His creation bracelet draws its inspiration from the maze motif found in Tohono O'odham basketry. It shows I'itoi (the Creator) emptying the maze of life, symbolizing creation, onto the land—everything pours forth, from water to insects to plants to humans to designs representing the life force of the land. This pattern is found as a petroglyph in many areas of the Sonoran Desert, which is the traditional home of the O'odham and their ancestors, the Hohokam. The design lends itself nicely to the path-of-life interpretation; while it has no shortcuts, there are no dead-ends either, and the entire path must be followed in order to complete the journey. Rick's visual variation on the maze has the man entering with a walking stick.

Over the years he has had a number of apprentices who have begun to follow his lead, with four—James Fendenheim, Chris José, Florine Morillo, and Kendrick Lopez—actively pursuing careers in silversmithing. Rick's journey as a silver artist continues as he gains inspiration for new designs, drawing upon ants and horned lizards, the plants used by basket weavers, the annual *bahidaj* or saguaro harvest, the life-giving summer rains …

Desert scene (above) and traditional maze pattern (below).

VICTOR LEE MASAYESVA
HOPI

VICTOR, A MEMBER OF THE SNAKE CLAN, lives just outside Hotevilla with his father, Ezra. Of his four sisters, two half-brothers, and one half-sister, only Victor and his half-brother Chalmers Day have gone into silverwork. The others have followed career paths that include teaching, counseling, and tribal justice.

Born in 1962, he attended high school in Ganado, Arizona, graduating in 1980. He was promptly hired by Ferrell and Dorothy Secakuku, then owners of the Hopi Cultural Center restaurant and hotel on Second Mesa. He was tired of school and wanted to buy a car and earn extra money, so he not only signed on to do maintenance work during the day, he waited tables and cooked at night. He credits the Secakukus with teaching him an important lesson: "to treat people as though they were my mom and dad."

After a year-and-a-half of this intense level of work, he applied to and was accepted at the Institute of American Indian Art in Santa Fe. "I went for a two-dimensional design and painting major," he says. "I took one class in jewelry, with Skip Holbrook. He taught silverwork starting from the very, very basics. Skip Holbrook was a pain in the butt," he says with a big smile. "He made me draw my own wire, roll my own sheet, and make my own stamping tools. Even make many of my own findings"—valuable skills that not many silversmiths have. "I only took it [the class] so I could make money, as I had no scholarship then. It wasn't until later that I got a Hopi tribal scholarship."

Like most beginners, he started working in copper. In a short time he was selling to staff at IAIA as well as to the IAIA museum. Beginning with overlay, he soon was experimenting with hollowware, creating a necklace of cloud and swirling water motifs. He also experimented with channel work, including a buckle set with wood, turquoise, and fossilized ivory. "Those things Skip taught us were things he said would come in handy someday if we found ourselves out there without machinery or a supply shop. Kind of like algebra—'someday you will find this useful,'" Victor laughs. "But then one day I found myself without those things, taking care of my mom [Laverne Cooka], who was on dialysis and very sick back home. I started by doing cut-out work, which didn't require any soldering."

While at IAIA, he says, "I tried to learn how to paint, but I never learned how to mix colors ... and painting was my major. I eventually passed with flying colors, but I feel that what I did learn I learned from [instructors] Joe Maktima and Ferrel Cockrum."

Victor attended the California College of Arts and Crafts in Oakland and was recognized as a Truman Scholar. While there, in the photo and print studio, he met George Rivera from Pojoaque, and the two became friends, writing their applications for the Truman scholarship together, helping each other out. George studied photography and ceramics. "He enjoyed the freedom of movement in clay and created vessels as large as four feet high," says Victor. "One night we went through like a hundred bowls so I could get the shape right and *finally* I got it. And George slashed it. I was stunned. I asked him why, and he said, 'Well, if you can do it once you can do it again.'"

Shortly after his first child, daughter Bertina, was born, he went to work at the Indian Pueblo Cultural Center in Albuquerque with John Mihelsic. "That was the fall of '85," he recalls. "I was there seven-and-a-half years, working in retail, managing the restaurant, doing marketing, working in the wholesale division, doing road sales, shows, overseas marketing, and training artists to do their own marketing." He left the IPCC in 1992 and by the following year he was working jewelry back home at Hopi, looking after his mother, making sure she made her dialysis appointments.

Searching for a new approach to Hopi jewelry, he sought advice from Bob Rhodes and Verma Nequatewa. They showed Victor how to texture silver with a roller and gave him a two-by-six-inch sheet of 18-gauge silver that had been run through the roller with a piece of sandpaper. "I ran home from their place all fired up and made pendants and earrings using turtle, rain cloud, and very geometric Kokopellis and took them back to show them the next day," he says. "That was 1993, and I did that style for nearly a decade."

In jewelry-making there are a lot of tricks and techniques to be learned, and it isn't uncommon to learn at least a few of them by trial and error. Victor happened to mention to Bob and Verma that he had run through a couple dozen or more jeweler saw blades while cutting out his first work. Most smiths doing that type of work use beeswax to lubricate the blade, so they asked him what kind of wax he was using. "I just kind of went 'Huh? Wax?' And then I started using beeswax and the problem stopped," he chuckles.

Unable to purchase a rolling mill and perhaps inspired by the self-reliance that Holbrook taught him, or perhaps moved by sheer necessity, Victor started out texturing his silver by taping a piece of sandpaper to the sheet silver and hammering it. He then thought to cast a thin sheet in cuttlebone, but found that the texture of the cuttlebone was too uniform and created texture in the silver that was too regular and impossible to vary. Again Bob Rhodes stepped in, suggesting he try some tufa, a sample of which Rhodes provided. "In tufa you have to be thinking ahead about your texture, but you can do a lot with it," says Victor. By 1997 his work shifted from cutout to overlay, a technique he still favors, but using an ever-changing array of textures. His hallmark, which he began using in 1995, is a lightning bolt.

Of his three kids, only Victor Bennett, who headed into the Navy at age eighteen in 2005, makes jewelry. In joining the Navy he follows in the footsteps of both grandfathers, who left this parched, high desert to serve at sea. Youngest daughter Brittany seems not tempted by jewelry-making, but his other daughter, Britina (b. 1985), entered beadwork in the Santa Fe Indian Market when she was thirteen.

For some time Victor has volunteered with the Red Feather Foundation, building straw-bale homes on the Northern Cheyenne Reservation. It is work that Victor finds important and gratifying; he has helped them open a satellite office in Bakavi Village and build homes at Hopi.

WAYNE MUSKETT
NAVAJO

DURING RODEO SEASON it's hard catching up with Wayne Muskett. He was born to the Haltsooí (Meadow) Clan and for the Bit'ahnii (Folding Arms) Clan in Gallup in 1971 to Etheline and Wilbert Muskett Sr. Since childhood, Wayne has spent much of his life in the saddle. He began calf-roping competitively about 1993. "We used to follow my brother-in-law to rodeos," he says. "You kind of get tired of watching, so I wanted to try it myself. Kind of how I started silver, watching my dad and then trying it myself." He now goes to every rodeo held on the eastern half of the Navajo reservation and any other rodeo, besides that, that he can find the time to get to. "I even win a few," he grins. That is the other thing you notice about Wayne right off: he loves to laugh, joke, and tease.

His brother, Wilbur Jr., makes jewelry, as do his four brothers-in-law. "They caught on," he laughs. His uncles make jewelry and so does his father, using the hallmark "W.M." and working in a more traditional style—different from the inlay work for which Wayne is known.

He started making jewelry in 1989, picking up some tips from his brother the year before. "My first customers were my high school teachers," he recalls. He graduated from Tohatchi High School in 1991. He didn't start signing his work, however, until 1993, when he had his current hallmark, MUSKETT, made.

Like most silversmiths, he found soldering the hardest. The small silver frames that separate the stone inlay work can't take as much heat as the heavier bracelet shank they are soldered into, and they must be perpendicular to the back of the bracelet so that the inlay

can be cut for a tight fit, so it takes a careful, experienced touch. "I used to start with ten bracelets and end up with nine," he says.

He started out making bola ties and pendants. As he learned the trick of forming bracelets, his father stepped in and helped dome the bracelets. The inlay work is the most time-consuming. After cutting the stones to fit and epoxying them into place, Wayne works the surface down with an 800-grit abrasive, then polishes it, rewashes it, checks it for any remaining scratches, then buffs it with Zam, polishes it, and checks it again.

He uses a wide range of material in his inlay work—turquoise from all over the world, coral, spondylus shell, tigereye, jet, charoite from Siberia, sugilite from the Kalahari, lapis from Afghanistan, gaspeite from Australia—and he's always looking for new, interesting material to set in his sterling and 14-karat gold jewelry.

He primarily wholesales his work. "I do one show a year" in San Diego, he says. "Wish I could do more shows. When you do too much jewelry sometimes you get tired of it. That's where rodeo comes in," he grins. He doesn't team rope "because team ropers often have damage to their hands, and I need my hands for jewelry!"

He and his wife, Darcia, a banker, have a daughter, Calesia (b. 1993). She is an accomplished barrel racer who wants to learn how to make jewelry, so the Muskett jewelry-making tradition seem pretty certain of continuing.

FARRON NAKA'WAYWISA
HOPI

BORN FARRON LOMAVITU IN 1968 to Virginia Nuvamsa and Louigi Lomavitu, this silversmith has called Ross Joseyesva "father" since he was one year old, and grew up using his last name. He has recently taken his initiation name of Naka'waywisa for his last name. This is a common occurrence at Hopi, where by traditional practice one had a single name, not a first and last, and that single name could and frequently did change over the course of one's life. One is given many names at birth and additional names after initiation(s), and one might be known by different names to different people—to the everlasting exasperation of an American bureaucracy that decreed names were composed of a first name and a family name.

Farron's father, Ross, worked silver, having learned at the Hopi Guild. Farron also learned his craft at the Guild, but his path was a little different. It began with ABC Welding School in Phoenix (he graduated from Phoenix Indian High School in 1986). A motorcycle accident in which he lost a leg forced his return to Hopi in 1989. To earn money he turned to katsina carving, primarily the sculptural style that represents the katsina spirit rather than the katsina dancer. In 1991 the Guild started a new class for silversmiths, and Farron responded to urgings to enroll. There he learned from Hopi smiths Charleston Lewis, Shannon Lamson, and Steve Kuyvaya. As most silversmiths will admit, soldering is the toughest skill to master, especially with the level of detail that Farron was drawn to in his design work. He finished his training and continued to work for the Guild until 1994. He then started working on his own in Steve Kuyvaya's workshop, along with Shannon Lamson and Charleston Lewis.

His hallmark at the beginning was simply "FJ." Later, the Guild ordered a hallmark he designed of a frog with a tadpole in the belly. (His uncle Wilmer Saufkie has a similar frog hallmark, but with a rain cloud in the belly.) And speaking of polliwogs, Farron and his wife, Ernestine Holmes (daughter of another well-known silversmith, Emory Holmes), have a son, Evan, a wriggly two years old at the time of our interview (2006).

Unlike many silversmiths, Farron's introduction to gold was entirely self-motivated. He decided to try it out and bought the gold on his own. His first effort, in 1998, was a silver ring, 7/8 inch wide, with a 14-karat gold sun symbol in the center. Because of its lower melting point, gold is tricky for a silversmith to master immediately, but according to Farron the first one "came out perfect! The second one didn't—the sun shifted off-center when it was being soldered." Another reason silversmiths are reluctant to work in gold: when something goes wrong you generally have to scrap the entire piece, and the price you receive for scrap gold is significantly less than you pay for gold sheet and wire.

"I was taught not to copy other people's work," he says. "If you use someone's idea you have to vary it, interpret it, change it somehow." Ironically, a few years ago he lost a prize to a copy of his work. He has sought to stay ahead of the copyists, Indian and non-Indian, with innovative, imaginative designs.

"I knew no one was making planets, so I tried one out in a bracelet in 1995," he says. "That first one had the solar system—sun and nine planets. When I finished, I was real excited; it was going to make me famous and I wanted to be known for my work." A godbrother who was initiated into the Wuwutsim (a Hopi men's religious society) saw the finished work and told him he'd made it the right (Hopi) way.

He plans each piece meticulously. "I draw out in detail, mainly where I want the planets first, then draw in a comet or shooting star. Sketch in stars and then start cutting them out." Two years later his work shifted from the night skies, planets, and stars to oceans and dolphins—fitting motifs for a member of the Water Clan.

His first exposure to selling to shops came when he traveled to Sedona with friends. "I started selling to Garland's first. I went down with Steve and Charley to Garland's where they sold their work. I took my jewelry just in case. And they bought us out. All of us!" More recently, through fellow artist Duane Lomayestewa, he found his first Japanese buyer, one of several who came out two or even three times a year to buy jewelry for their shops in Japan.

Farron used to sell his work at some of the smaller Indian art shows, mostly in Arizona, but he is now opening his own small shop/workshop called Hotòmqam/Soongwuqam at milepost 381 just outside Songoopavi Village. The first part of the name refers to the Milky Way as seen during the winter solstice, and the second is the Milky Way as seen in summer. The name reflects his lifelong interest in astronomy: "I always wanted to know what is out there."

ALBERT NELLS
NAVAJO

ALTHOUGH ALBERT WAS BORN IN WINSLOW, ARIZONA, in 1953, he and his six brothers and two sisters were raised near Cedar Springs, Arizona. One brother carves fetishes, and a couple of siblings have worked in silver in the past, but Albert is the only one working in silver full-time.

Albert, born to the Salt ('Áshiihí) Clan and for the Folding Arms (Bit'ahnii) Clan, did leatherwork all through high school to earn money. He graduated from high school at Many Farms, Arizona, in 1972 and went on to learn silverwork. Self-taught, Albert observed that learning silver wasn't too hard because of his experience with leather tooling. "With leatherwork you have to do your best each time, because when you make a hole or stamp or a design you can't undo it," he says.

His first work was not unlike that created by many Navajo silversmiths using silver, coral, and turquoise. It was not until the early 1980s that he developed his own distinctive style. "One day I was sitting there thinking about what I would put together and that got me to thinking about Navajo rug designs, especially old saddle blankets and how they made the border for protection. I asked questions from elders, and it always kept coming back to the same thing: rug designs and the border for protection—borders that go from point to point to point. Like sun rays that reflect certain points. That's how it really came about, you see. You see the same design, that border, in pottery, in saddle blankets, in sandpaintings, too. And different tribes use it, too, but in different ways."

As a part of his new style he began to inlay coral, turquoise, jet, and white shell. "Those colors represent the four directions, the four mountains that mark our land. For those colors I use only the traditional materials, the ones mentioned in our stories—never lapis or other stones."

His new work quickly gained a following. "I first started selling at retail shows, mostly museum shows. Then to your shop [Bahti Indian Arts] and then a couple more in Santa Fe. Now I sell to about ten to twelve stores."

Though best known for his silverwork, he does some items in gold. Albert started working in gold about fifteen years ago—it was for a special order and was a solid gold piece. But even today he works gold only on special order.

He began to enter competitions for the exposure it gave him to the buying public. He never looks at competition as going against anyone. "I (enter competitions) for the public," he says. "They are the ones who compare, who really judge. A ribbon is merely the icing on the cake. I limit myself in competitions, because everything I do belongs to the Holy People."

Like other silversmiths, he is aware that exposing your work in competitions draws attention to your design and can result in imitations. But, like most of the better silversmiths working today, he says that the best protection from copies is the quality of his work.

His wife, Marylou, and his kids, "they help a little bit—mostly with the cleanup. My wife and kids call me 'expert' and don't even want to help me," he says, laughing.

His youngest daughter is starting to draw and paint, and the kids are in junior rodeo, following the lead of their father, who did some rodeoing while in high school, riding broncs and bulls.

Albert used to travel a lot to stores and shows across the Southwest but has found that increasingly expensive (as have many Indian artists), so currently he restricts his participation to shows at the Heard Museum in Phoenix and the Santa Fe Indian Market. It limits the opportunity to meet the people who appreciate his work, but it also gives him more time to create the work that is so admired.

GIBSON NEZ
JICARILLA APACHE/NAVAJO

GIBSON WAS BORN IN 1947 at Dulce, New Mexico, on the Jicarilla Apache Reservation. His mom, Mary Bicenti, was a Jicarilla rancher. At age fifty, she went back to school to earn a bachelor's degree in public administration and became a tribal judge. Jake Nez, his Navajo father, also ranched.

Of five boys (all of whom are fluent in both Navajo and Apache), Gibson is the oldest. Largely raised by their mom, the five brothers sorely tested her judicial temperament with the kind of pranks one might expect from five boys on a ranch, but it is safe to say her guidance prevailed.

Gibson never got his high school diploma because, he says, "I started chasing rodeo when I was fourteen. Got my PRCA [Professional Rodeo Cowboy Association] card when I was sixteen and figured that was a better deal. I did a lot of leatherwork, stampwork, while I was rodeoing, something I learned when I was twelve years old in 4-H at high school. On the rodeo circuit I was making and selling chaps, cutting [spur] rowels out of steel, making bootstraps … always trying to figure out a way to make enough money to get to the next town and the next rodeo."

He used to ride bulls, but "when I turned about twenty-five I started riding broncs. In 1974 I was nineteenth in the nation. AIRCA [American Indian Rodeo Cowboy Association] started about '65 or so, and I got a card from them and was inducted into the Indian Cowboy Hall of Fame in 1982. My last ride was in, I think it was '86. That was in Denver

City, Texas. Still got that buckle." He adds, "I was the first Southwest Indian to win at Crow Fair in Pryor, Montana, in 1974."

In 1976 Gibson started working with silver full-time. "I used to run around with Sammy Saavedra, and he showed me how to work with silver, how to solder," he says. "I made chaps for him, and he showed me the ropes. It came natural to me, probably because of all the leatherwork I did. I used to go to galleries and study other people's work and see how it was made. That was my education."

His first entry into a jewelry competition was the 1977 New Mexico State Fair, where a buckle and bola tie set won first prize. (It sold for a modest $150.) Traveling and sleeping in his green Impala, he made the rounds through the Southwest, entering shows and selling his work.

It was not the best time to start working silver: the metal had hit $35 an ounce and was climbing still. But as Gibson observes, "It's not so much the price [of your materials] as what you do with it." And what he did with it clearly impressed those who saw the finished work.

He took his buffer and his silversmithing stump on the bus to Gallup and then to Farmington. "Franklin Sandoval, who often supported me during my rodeo career, was mayor of Farmington at the time. I got a $5,000 loan for materials from him. Then my brother Julian and I hitchhiked to Santa Monica, California, to a big show there. Betty Benally from the Navajo Guild let us sell our work from her booth. Money was tight—we even washed out our clothes on the beach. Then Sunday came. Yetta, from a shop called Turquoise Lady, came and bought everything we had: $13,000 worth. Forget the bus; we *flew* back, paid back Franklin plus $1,000, and I was on my way."

Two years later his work made the 1979 *Arizona Highways* collector's edition. "I went by Joe Tanner's store, and he showed me the issue. That was the first I knew of it." Before long he was selling to a number of high-end shops and museum gift shops, the Heard Museum and the Museum of Northern Arizona being the first. "That issue changed my life," he says. "I was even able to sell the green Impala that was my bedroom," he laughs. "I sold it to Yetta.

"I use only the best turquoise I can find. When I was starting out I'd buy Stormy Mountain turquoise from Clyde Wright, Blue Diamond and Nevada Blue from Ron Hammond, and Lone Mountain spiderweb from Francis Fare and the Winfields." Good stone, good clean work, heavy-gauge silver, and all-handmade findings are what he describes as the backbone of his work. And it has paid off for him: in 1982, for example, "I entered 125 pieces of jewelry in shows and won 65 blue ribbons, and best of show in silver and best of show, for a total of $15,000 in ribbon money."

Gibson started his distinctive inlay work of the edges of his jewelry in the early 1980s. Favored motifs of his include a stepped design from Jicarilla baskets and a Navajo sun design. Over time, he observes, his work has gone from the more traditional to a contemporary style, merging the feelings of the two approaches.

He used a hallmark from the get-go, using his mom's cattle brand and, as a precaution against would-be imitators, he registered his hallmark as a trademark with the state of New Mexico.

He is quite proud of the fact that many celebrities have purchased his work. It started when "this one guy named James Katz, from L.A., president of Universal Pictures Classics, was shooting *Lust in the Dust*. He was looking for jewelry. He found out about my work and sent a limo for me to take me to the set, and I sold to a lot of the stars and movie people there. Bette Midler, Lainie Kazan, Calvin Klein—they all own my work. I got invited to Goldie Hawn's Christmas party one year and Goldie bought some of my work. It just spread by word-of-mouth. Also, [Navajo] Chairman MacDonald owns my work, and he introduced me to Lorne Greene and Pernell Roberts, who also bought my work."

He pauses in his recollections to scratch the ears of his old dog Rufus, a gift from Robert Redford. "Rufus has been with me for twelve years. Heck, when I go places, people call out for *him,* not me," he says with his famous grin.

Helped by others in his career, he has attempted to pass on that generosity of spirit, helping out younger silversmiths as they have come up, including Byron McCurtin (Kiowa), Dillon Chiago (Salt River Pima), and James Fendenheim (Tohono O'odham).

Among the silversmiths whose work Gibson admires is Jake Livingston, with whom he traveled early in his career, and who mentored him. Gibson also praises Thomas Curtis and Lee Yazzie, "who was ahead of his time. I put him on a pedestal." And a lot of people put Gibson's work on one, too.

LOREN PANTEAH AND YOLANDA LAATE
ZUNI

ABOVE: *Bola clasp by Celestine Cooche, grandfather of Loren Panteah.*

"SOME OF THE DESIGNS COME IN MY DREAMS and I remember what they look like when I wake up, and I tell it to Loren and he draws it out," says Yolanda Laate. She and Loren Panteah have created several dozen designs since they first began to work together.

Loren, born into his mother's Badger Clan and his father's Bear Clan in 1960, started out carving the small stone and shell animals commonly called fetishes—but that was before he discovered motorcycles. While in high school he got "too attached to the motorcycles; that is where most of my money went," he laughs. He took up jewelry-making, learning from his mother, Susie Laweka. He remembers soldering being the hardest skill to master. (Loren and Yolanda's youngest daughter, Lynse Laate, would probably agree. The only one of their three children to work silver, she makes plain silver pieces that do not require soldering.)

Loren's mother and her parents were doing clusterwork, and that is the style Loren, too, began to make, continuing an old family tradition. "My late grandparents, Celestine and Elizabeth [Cooche], used to sell their work various places, including setting up on the roadside in Farmington during fair time" and in Gallup during the famed Gallup Intertribal Ceremonial.

But jewelry-making remained a part-time activity, a way of earning money to support himself as he worked toward his goal, earning a degree in wildlife biology at the University of New Mexico. (He is currently employed by the Zuni Division of Natural Resources.)

Yolanda, or Yo, born into the Corn Clan in 1959, is sister to Sylvia Hooee (see page 52) and the daughter of Juan and Lyla Tsethlikai, jewelers well known for their petit-point work. "All I did when I was in high school was the silver drops to help our mom," says Yolanda. "I cut silver into strips to heat up and make balls, and then pounded them a little flat so they wouldn't roll. She used them to set around her work. I didn't start my own work until the 1980s. In 1979 we had our first child, and I was a mother. We moved to Las Cruces with Loren while he went to school there, then came back about 1983. At the time we came back, jobs were scarce and we had no choice but to work with silver, so we started making different designs, and began selling it.

"Our first design had a sun face in the center with a star design around the outside. We started using different colors when we made the star part, for variety. It took me a while to do the centerpiece exactly right, centered just so—to even it out. We piece the mosaic together first, then grind it smooth. We drill holes for the eyes and mouth so we can inlay them. It's hard to keep the drill bit from skittering around at first—you have to hold it

steady, but once you get the hang of it it's easier." Smiling at Loren, she acknowledges that "Loren was doing the drilling. And he's the one that did the silverwork." But in 1998 she tried doing some silverwork. "I made about six pieces and sold them all during an artist-studio-tour presentation and demonstration we were doing with New Mexico State University's Elderhostel Program."

Most of their work, however, had sold to traders and shops rather than directly to the public at shows. That changed in 1994 when they participated in the Eight Northern Pueblos Show, where artists had the opportunity to sell direct. "After the show we realized we hadn't sold as many pieces but had more money! We were so excited." From there they went on to participate in a number of juried art shows.

As the quality of their work and the designs continued to improve and evolve, the demand increased and many took notice. "One trader, Turquoise Village, offered to sell our work for more, and pay us more. I was doing most of the selling, but this one time I let Loren sell them. So when he took them in and came back, he said that guy cheated himself—'Look at what he paid us!'"

But with fame come copy artists. Recalls Yo, "About 1992 we saw a large copy of an original jewelry design of ours at the Albuquerque State Fair. It happened because we wouldn't sell large lots of jewelry for less to a certain trader, so he hired someone to copy them. And so there was someone else's name on the back of this piece. It turned out the guy was a Navajo silversmith living in Fort Defiance [Arizona] who didn't know what was happening, that he had been asked to copy our work."

Loren continues, "We started thinking of protecting our own designs. In '95 I saw a newspaper clipping where the Hopi had approached the Arizona state legislature about protecting their arts and crafts, where wholesalers supported them. From there on I wanted something similar to that to protect Zuni arts and crafts. Octavius Seotewa and I approached our tribal council and Governor Donald Eriacho about what they can do to protect Zuni arts and crafts."

The tribe formed a Zuni trademark committee at their recommendation, and seven individuals (including Seotewa and Panteah) were appointed to the committee, meeting quarterly, consulting trademark lawyers, doing research. As members of ZCAC (Zuni Cultural Arts Council), the committee had also been working with the tribe to set up a certification mark to protect against copies of Zuni jewelry. Essentially it would be a tribally owned mark with each Zuni user certified by the tribe before he or she could use it. With their efforts, the tribe passed the "Certification for Zuni Made Arts and Crafts Ordinance," and in January 2006 Loren, Carlton Jamon, and Tony Eriacho were appointed by the tribe as commissioners to develop and implement the ordinance and help protect the work that has sustained many families like theirs at Zuni and may be able to continue to sustain them, economically and aesthetically, into the future.

ALLEN POOYOUMA
HOPI

HOPI JEWELRY ARTIST ALLAN POOYOUMA is one of those silversmiths who is a link to another era. Even as a young man, he was a talented silversmith who, like a select number of his peers, could find work in almost any city. In the 1930s, 40s, and 50s, Hopi and Navajo silversmiths traveled, worked, and lived in cities across the Southwest, from Los Angeles to Denver. They found work by word-of-mouth from one silversmith to another, and relied on recommendations from fellow silversmiths (to whom they were often related by blood, marriage, or clan).

Born in 1922 to Gene Nuvahoyouma and Vera Pooyouma in the village of Hotevilla, he is of the Cloud and Corn Clans. (Hotevilla was founded in 1906 after the village of Orayvi split over whether to cooperate with the Americans or keep their own traditions. The conservatives lost and had to leave that winter, founding the new village.) He has one older brother, Rex, who worked for many years as a moccasin-maker for the late Ben MacMillan at the Kaibab Shop in downtown Tucson, the same city where Allen would find work as a silversmith.

Allen was one of a generation of Hopis forcibly taken from their families and sent to school many miles away. He and Rex were taken away by policemen on horseback in the midst of a religious observance. "We were still dancing with the Katsinas, my mother making baskets," he recalls. "They took us to day school. When we get there they cut our hair. The teachers were all white.

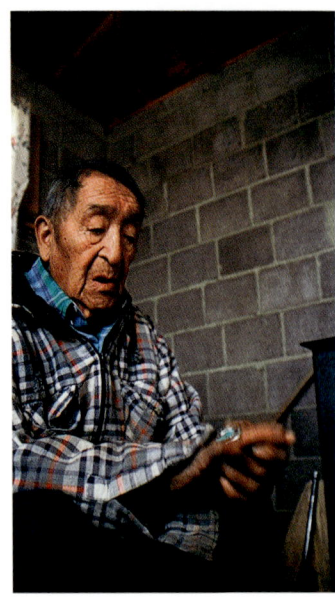

"I learned [silversmithing] from my father and my uncle Ralph [Tawangyaouma, 1906–1973]. It was hammer-and-file work first. I think I started when I was fifteen [1937]. I was helping my father and my *ta'ah* [uncle]. They sold mostly just to other Hopis." The change in the subsistence economy among the Hopis was evident even at that relatively early date, as he relates that they sold to other Hopis for money, not for trade. Much of their jewelry was set with turquoise that they bought in both rough and cut form.

Most silversmiths, even those self-taught, usually arrived at similar, if not the same, solutions to various aspects of silverwork, but occasionally you hear of surprisingly unique solutions or techniques, such as the way Allen learned to make the silver drops (sometimes called "raindrops") that embellish much of Indian silver jewelry. "At that time my father showed me how to make raindrops: melt silver in a cup and—throw it on the floor! We pick out the sizes we want and sort them." The idea of molten silver being flung on the floor is a bit daunting, but Allen assured me that it worked, though it works best if you "throw it right."

"The first things I made were rings—most just plain silver. I used square [silver] slugs, melted, then hammered them. It took four for a bracelet. Used a chisel instead of a saw to cut them out. First time I used a saw was when I was twenty-five"—almost a decade after he first started silversmithing. He began using his Corn Clan hallmark sometime after World War II, when the Hopi Guild was set up to train Hopi silversmiths under the GI Bill. Its Hopi founders, Fred Kabotie and Paul Saufkie, encouraged each silversmith to design and use a hallmark, frequently based upon a clan symbol or using the smith's initials. Allen, already an experienced smith of two decades, did not attend Guild classes, but the push for hallmarks did reach him. As he remembers it, "I started using a hallmark after government told us to."

But to earn a living he turned to construction work, traveling around to where the work was. "I was at Grey Mountain when I was mixing mud for the people that lay stones. That's when they called me for the Army. I was with them at Grey Mountain for one week, then I went to Phoenix. There was about three of us [Hopis] from Hotevilla and about four from Polacca and about two from Bakavi. And I don't know how many from Lower Orayvi. I had a bad eye on one side. They sent me back home and from there I went to Winslow. That's where I found work. On pipeline excavation—shovel and pick work. About a year there and then they laid me off, then I went back to Hotevilla. I was out there for two years with my parents. Then someone from Flagstaff came looking for a silversmith.

"I started working for Doc Williams, making rings, setting petrified wood. Two years with him and somebody looking for another silversmith comes from Ash Fork [west of Flagstaff], so I went with him. I was out there six months. Then I got lonesome. There was only three stores and the train stop. I got on a freight train and went through to Flagstaff. Next day I show up at Doc Williams's place and go back to work. There was

136 SILVER & STONE

another man, a boy that works with me there, Eddie Scott [Sr.—whom Allen taught]. We made nothing but rings with petrified wood."

After one more year there, "something came up" and he went back to Winslow and construction work, and the change of pace it provided. The following year found him back in Hotevilla. "I stayed there a couple months, and then my Uncle Ralph wants me to go to Tucson. He was working at the Santa Rita Hotel for Mr. [William] McDaniels. That's where I got a job." He started at $40 a week, working his way up to $50 by the time he left.

"I met a lot of movie actors there. John Wayne the most. Every time he goes out to film he comes back and comes by and tells me, 'I'm back—they didn't kill me yet!' I made John Wayne two hatbands, and he ordered three buckles for his friends. I used to get the special orders there. That's [also] where I get the saw for cutting silver instead of the chisel." Though he was frequently busy with special orders, if there were none, whatever else he made "they left up to me." He did quite a bit of repair work, but tried to avoid repairing Zuni pieces, with their tiny stonework. "I liked working with big stones only," he says. As his uncle did not make boxes and pillboxes, that fell to Allen. "I made one silver box, a large one for some movie actor. I have a hard time with that. But I make a lot of those pillboxes—square ones."

Allen kept his connection to his home at Hopi, going home each year at planting time, for the Niman Ceremony and for the annual Hopi Show in July at the Museum of Northern Arizona, where his wife made *piki* (a wafer-thin, blue-corn bread). Interjects his youngest son, Todd: "All of us kids sold piki bread. Back then we sold it for only 10 cents apiece. When we were young we were embarrassed by my parents dressing up traditional for that." Allen has four sons—Marvin, Steven, Larry, and Todd—of whom Larry and Steve work silver.

Though his uncle did some sand-cast work, Allen's standard techniques were stampwork and overlay. He left Tucson about 1970 when "some guy came down to the Santa Rita about a schoolteacher needed in Holbrook. My wife (Donna Lomatska) taught one year, second grade, in Tucson. So we left. My uncle left a few years before."

Approaching ninety, he continues to work silver, making what he likes, when he likes. Asked about the new styles and techniques that have evolved over the six decades since he first started working silver, he is polite but candid: "Well, sometimes I like them, but sometimes I don't."

ANGIE REANO OWENS AND FAMILY
SANTO DOMINGO PUEBLO

THE INTERVIEW WITH ANGIE BEGAN ON A SATURDAY, NOVEMBER 1, in the midst of Santo Domingo Pueblo's All Soul's Day feast. The house was awash in food, family, friends, guests, greetings, and laughter—a lot of laughter. The walls were hung with paintings she has traded for over the years. You could hear the religious dances out in the nearby plaza, while across from Angie's house was a kitchen from which flowed a near-constant stream of bread, pies, coffee, and savory stews, tamales, and chili. In the room next to the kitchen was her workshop, where jewelry in various stages of completion lay, awaiting her attention in a less hectic time. The scene was a fair reflection of her life, her priorities, and her nature.

One of eight children, born in 1946 to Joe Isidro and Clara Lovato, Angie has a son, Dean, who works for the Bureau of Indian Affairs and does some jewelry-making, as does his wife, Rena Williams Owens (Navajo), who learned the craft from her mother-in-law. Angie's daughter, Donna Owens Carey, who lived in Montana, developed her own distinctive style of silverwork before she tragically died in an automobile accident in March of 2007. Donna (b. 1970) had moved to Montana at age eighteen, but not before learning how to work silver and turquoise. In an interview prior to her death, she said, "I started helping Mom when I was seven, when my brother and I started with learning how to glue the mosaics. Then we learned grinding. My brother started using the lapidary saw at age eight, but I was afraid of it so I waited a while," she laughed. "I loved doing the mosaic work when I was young, but it was intimidating working under my mother because she is *so* well known."

Angie's mother hired Stella Naranjo to teach her children how to work silver, "But I melted everything I turned my torch on." It wasn't until she was twenty-one that Angie returned to silverwork—and to mosaic work, developing her own style. She incorporates motifs from the pottery of her great-grandmother, Monica Silva, in her earrings, bracelets, and ranger buckles, along with mosaic work. And Donna's son Dalton (b. 1993) started out making copper bracelets and then in 2005 began working in silver, making stampwork crosses.

Angie Reano's oldest grandson, Daniel, is learning silversmithing, and the next youngest grandson, Corey, has been her apprentice since 2001—much as Angie learned, under her mother's supervision, sitting at a small bench her father made, drilling shell blanks for beads. "We used to compete with each other to see who could make them the fastest," she recalls. She began jewelry-making on her own, with mosaics, in the late 1960s. "Our mom did mosaic on shell as a young woman. It died out and I thought I'd try that style first—on earrings. Me and my brother Percy sat down and figured it out," she says.

For an adhesive she has always used two-part epoxy for its durability. At one time she used to add chimney soot to create a black epoxy, but now she adds a mineral powder. About the mid-1970s she started inlaying in a herringbone style that has become her

signature. "How did it start I really don't know," she says. "One day I was just trying to make a design. Usually I went straight [with the mosaic] but that time I started to make a design that came out a herringbone."

Her work employs both green and blue turquoise. "It just depends upon whatever the traders bring in and looks like it would be good to use. Some of the nicest I used, but can't get anymore, had a brown matrix and was a nice blue, from the Kingman area. It cuts nice. Beautiful turquoise. Only once in a while does it crack." She notes that the price of some of her favorite turquoise has escalated over the years, from $45 a pound to $600. "I started using lapis, whenever it was first introduced … an Afghan diplomat brought some lapis during the fighting over there to Santa Fe, and that is where I got the first lapis I used. We *used* to use ivory, me and Percy, but if you use ivory in mosaic work it tends to separate from whatever you glue it with or glue it to—even if you first clean it with acetone, scratch it up and everything."

Generally Angie works with natural turquoise, but for earrings she will use stabilized turquoise; earrings are handled a lot, and natural turquoise subjected to soaps and oils from frequent handling will often change color, while stabilized or treated turquoise will not. As for the availability of good turquoise, she observes that "if the stones are meant for you, you will be there when they are there." That happened fairly recently when she found and bought a Persian turquoise necklace at an antique store. "It was beauuuuutiful turquoise—I sliced a piece and saw just how beautiful." And what project is she is saving it for? She just smiles.

She meticulously finishes the surface of her inlay work—from the grinder to a 100-grit sander, then 220, then 400, and then 600, before polishing with Zam and then a white diamond paste.

She began setting some of her mosaic work, previously done on shell, in silver in the 1970s, eventually designing and using a hallmark that represents a tiny shell mosaic, but she quit setting the work in silver in the early 1980s, in part because "if you use mosaic in metal you are in competition with all kinds of people."

For a while, as an alternative hallmark Angie would set a small turquoise bead in the back of her mosaics, but she stopped the practice after a little bit: "Phooey! If they want my bracelet they have to take my word for it," she laughs, adding, "There is something about putting a hallmark on my work. … I wasn't brought up to put that trademark. It is just a part of the tradition I was raised in." Her son Dean uses "DEO" as his hallmark; grandson Daniel uses "DO," and daughter Donna Owen Carey used "DOC."

Angie's jewelry is well known and highly recognizable. "I usually don't wear my own jewelry, but I was wearing it in New York City and someone recognized it, and then in Flagstaff I was at a gas station and this Gallup lady recognized the work. She said, 'Those are made by Angie Reano—do you know her?' I said, 'I guess I do.'"

NICK AND ME-WEE ROSETTA
SANTO DOMINGO PUEBLO

NICK ROSETTA (B. 1951) IS ONE OF FIVE CHILDREN of Ray and Mary Rosetta, who are famous for their handmade silver tube necklaces, dubbed "liquid silver" for the fineness and fluid quality of the strands, a style of work they invented about 1958–59. Though small-diameter silver tubular beads had been incorporated into coral and turquoise bead necklaces before, no one had made a necklace of *only* handmade tube beads, and none had ever been so finely made. According to Nick, the necklace style was christened by the wife of longtime Indian arts dealer Ed Young of Albuquerque, who marveled at the quality of work, drawing the necklace through her fingers and exclaiming, "It's like liquid silver!"

All the children—Nick, Johnny (d. 2003), Bruce, Joe, and Pablita—helped their folks make the necklaces, but their first job was not cutting the sheet silver into thin strips, nor was it drawing the strips through progressively smaller holes in a draw plate until the sheet became tubes, nor cutting the tubes, nor tediously polishing and smoothing the ends of each bead; it was stringing. Each strand, says Nick, "had to run from our dad's shoulder to the fingertips: twenty-five inches, and that meant 640 pieces, so we strung by count. It would take all day to do five to seven strings."

"Back in those days," Nick notes wistfully, "a full sheet of silver cost about $20–$30." They then "got an old cottonwood stump, pounded a long indentation or groove into it, took an old claw hammer, and used the ends to draw along the strip of silver to make it half round … pre-shape it." Then began the process of pulling the strips into tubes. "You have to use wax in final draws," he explains. "It takes five pulls on 28-gauge but sixteen pulls on [the heavier] 20-gauge. I get little grooves on my thumb after fifteen–twenty of them."

Nick graduated from Bernalillo High School in 1970 and woke up in his dad's truck the next morning to find that his dad's 16-gauge shotgun had been stolen while he was sleeping. "I figured I was in real hot water and needed to do something—so I joined the Navy the next day. I didn't even tell my folks—by 4:30 a.m. the following day I was on a plane headed to Orlando. I was in the service for six years. I was stationed in the Philippines, where people thought I was a Filipino—a *tall* Filipino," he laughs.

"When I got out I had a job waiting for me in Dallas, but Dad said, 'You've been gone too long. Time to come home.' So I did." Nick's day job now is as the master electrician/lighting technician at the Museum of Natural History in Albuquerque, where he has worked for many years.

Nick describes his wife, Me-Wee (b. 1948), as "calm, mellow." He remembers the very day he first saw her: December 12, 1967. "There was a dance at the community center, and I saw this girl in a brown dress with yellow polka dots." Me-Wee Garcia was an experienced bead-maker, which she'd learned from working with her grandfather, Tomasito Tenorio, making joclas and tab necklaces. Together they have two sons, named Robert and Oliver, and two daughters, Petra and Orojia.

With Nick, Me-Wee "had to get used to doing the small work," Nick says. "Right now she is doing all the stringing and designing of the necklaces." Asked what the most demanding part of the job is for him, Nick immediately responds, "Grinding is the toughest. I keep track of bead size and consistency by relying on feel. I do it with my eyes closed. As it goes through my fingertips I can tell if it is high and I should go slow or zip on through. I work on a whole strand at one time—twenty-six inches. Turquoise is the hardest material to work with; if I start with twenty-six inches, I lose four inches to breakage."

Grandson Mariano seems the one most likely to continue the family tradition. Another grandson, Josiah, age three, nicknamed "Josiah No-knuckles" and described by his doting grandfather as "the terror of the house," has had his hand in jewelry-making too, but not quite the way that Grandpa Nick was hoping. "He takes and hides my stuff. Sometimes it's my tools, like he did a couple weeks ago. I had thirty-three strips of silver ready to pull that I couldn't find. I been looking for them almost half the year, then I was looking for some other stuff I had lost in the back shed. I had a sack of structolite and I thought 'Could he …? Nah.' But I dug in there and looked and there they were!" Perhaps in time Josiah will join Mariano in following in their family's footsteps, *making* jewelry instead of hiding it.

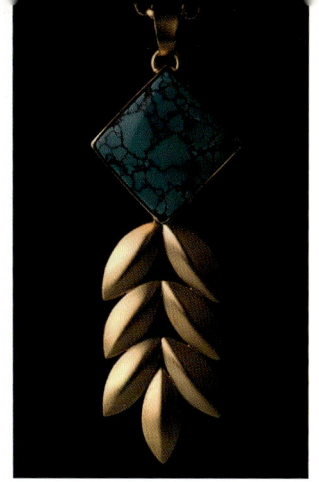

MARIA SAMORA
TAOS PUEBLO

THOUGH HER MOTHER MADE JEWELRY AT ONE TIME, it is fair to say that jewelry-making found Maria rather than the other way around. "One of my girlfriends, after getting back from college, asked if I wanted to take a course with her at UNM–Taos," she remembers. "I said, 'Sure, what do you want to take?' It was a jewelry course."

The daughter of Chien Motto, an Indiana native drawn to the magic of Taos during youthful wandering, and Frank Samora of Taos Pueblo, Maria Samora was born in Taos in 1975. After graduating from high school in 1993 she attended Pitzer College, where she studied fine arts, photography, and Spanish before traveling and living in South America.

Returning to Taos in 1997, she took that fateful jewelry class, learning soldering, filing, and a few other basic skills, "but enjoying it a lot. I figured I needed to study it seriously, so I signed up for an intensive class at the Taos Institute of Art with a goldsmith named Phil Poirier. Two days into the class I asked if I could apprentice with him. He hedged, but that fall I started and worked with him for the next six years. The first project he gave me required soldering something like 2,000 gold jump-rings, and I had never even worked with gold."

Part of her apprenticeship included studying books of the works of a wide range of jewelry masters, with Cartier's work especially resonating with her. By 1998 she had begun to make her own jewelry, but it was another four years before she began showing at a gallery. Instead she continued to work as a waitress at Lambert's restaurant in Taos, wearing her jewelry creations. Diners often admired them and occasionally "they would buy a

piece right off me." A frequent diner and former neighbor, Leroy Garcia, kept asking about her work, expressing an interest in it. Husband Kevin was also an important presence, encouraging her to strike out on her own, full-time. By 2002 she agreed to show her work in Garcia's Blue Rain Gallery.

"I started out working in silver—it was all I could afford—and then later began to combine it with gold. Recently I started working in solid gold. From my training with Phil I have developed a preference for heavy bezels, usually 18-gauge. That means setting the stones with careful hammer work instead of burnishing. And that can crack the stone if you aren't careful." She works with a wide range of stones and precious stones, including turquoise, moonstones, garnets, diamonds, pearls, black star dioxide, rose quartz, chalcedony … whatever catches her fancy.

Her first entry into Indian Market was in 2005. She came away with a second prize for a contemporary gold bracelet. A distinguishing feature of Maria's jewelry is an ancient Incan coloring technique. "I alloy my own gold," she says. She uses naturally occurring acids to deplete the surface, leaving the gold with the subtle luster and richness of 24-karat, yet retaining the 18-karat durability. It's then bead-blasted for a softer, almost powdery visual texture. Maria's mother proudly notes that "her work is drawn from both Old World and New World metalworking techniques, influences, and heritage."

Currently she is experimenting and designing with bead chain, a material that caught her eye a little while ago. "It looked like fun material so I started playing around with it. The chain has been riveted and is so fine you can't attach it by soldering, so I use other methods."

Her father, who died in the summer of 2007 at age 101, was a quiet man; but at the time of my visit with Maria, as he gazed upon his children—Yellow Bird (Maria's older brother, a potter) and Maria—I could see the look of approval and pride in his eyes, which then looked toward the door to the next room, where the next generation, Maria's newborn son Quentin, lay sleeping.

CODY A. SANDERSON
NAVAJO

THE THIRD OF FIVE CHILDREN, Cody was born in 1964 in Gallup, New Mexico, to Anna Notah and Tommy Sanderson. Cody is enrolled with the Navajo tribe but is affiliated with Nambé Pueblo and, from his grandparents' generation, is of Hopi and Akimel O'odham (Pima) heritage. After graduating from Window Rock High in 1982, Cody studied at Mesa Community College and took summer classes at Arizona State University and Northern Arizona University. "Wherever I was, I tried to be a student of something," he says. By 1985, however, he decided to join the Navy. His intent was to be a corpsman because of his interest in medicine and be stationed on the West Coast, but the Navy had other plans for him; he went into the nuclear-propulsion program and was sent to the East Coast. He did tours of the Mediterranean and the Caribbean that were eventful, but he knew the Navy wasn't for him.

When he mustered out at Norfolk, Virginia, he headed inland to Window Rock and continued his education at the University of New Mexico's Gallup branch. And in conjunction with school, he trained as a chiropractic therapist. Though he did not become a chiropractor, more than one silversmith with a cramp in his back has come to Cody for help.

Moving to Santa Fe, finishing up some classes at Santa Fe Community College, and planning on starting chiropractic college, he wound up working as both a retail salesperson, at End of the Trail for Deborah Hudgins, and as a road salesman, for MM Rogers Company, for a total of nearly ten years. In his last year or so he acquired a damaged

silverworking bench and, little by little, silverworking tools. Ever the learner, he set about teaching himself silverworking, reading books and asking questions—lots of questions—of established metalsmiths.

The first technique he used was stampwork. "Of course it was crude and crooked … now it's just crooked but a lot more refined," he laughs. He used his own hallmark (an intertwined "CAS" in script) from the very beginning. "I think it elevates the piece. I usually add 'Santa Fe' and 'STERLING' as well."

Though no one in Cody's immediate family ever worked silver, "I always had an interest in it since I was real young. I started in the late 1990s manipulating silver to see what I could do with it. I started out in plain silver, no stones, and asked questions, a lot of questions. People who are well established and well up in the field were very free with their information. I am very grateful for their openness and willingness to help and try to reciprocate by doing the same for people who come to me."

One of the ways he does this is by working as a silversmithing instructor at the Poeh Center, where he himself once took classes. A quick study, he was a student there in 2001 and an instructor by 2002.

Among the silversmiths who have helped and advised him are Seth Norbeck, McKee Platero, David Gaussoin, and Steve Taylor. Cody also cites Kenneth Begay and Charles Loloma for their lack of fear in breaking through barriers and stereotypes; by doing so, they "opened the door for the next generation."

Cody recently moved out of his garage studio to a space within Seth Norbeck's large, spacious, and wonderfully equipped studio. (Among the wonders is the fact that it is warm in the winter and cool in the summer, rather than vice versa.)

His equipment runs the gamut from simple hammers to a new, state-of-the-art computer-assisted wax modeling machine. Cody enthusiastically embraces and explores the technology at his fingertips. "People don't have a problem with Natives having DVDs and microwaves; why shouldn't we also be able to use the newest technology in our art?" Among his equipment are two rolling mills (one electric, one hand-operated) and a machine that enables him to draw wire from the ingots he casts. "Buying wire is maybe cheaper and easier but when it's 2 a.m. and I need a piece of wire and everything is closed …"

Cody describes many of the pieces he creates using lost-wax casting techniques as "visually digestible—you know what they are and where they come from. Someone might say, 'Hey, this looks like Lego blocks,' and I say, 'That's because it is.'" These pieces, which start out as experiments, are derived from such diverse items as the wheel of a toy car, a monkey from a Barrel of Monkeys game, and the neck and cap of an airline liquor bottle. Some of these experiments are successful and become pieces of jewelry; others are, well, experiments. But even the most successful piece cannot be exhibited in most juried American Indian art shows because of restrictions against lost-wax cast multiples (up until

World War II, there were standards in place that said Indian jewelry could not be marked as handmade if any electric-powered equipment was used). A small but growing number of metalsmiths like Cody feel that allowing the technique would elevate and transform American Indian jewelry-making. "True, some jewelers will take advantage of it, but some will run with it and innovate," he says. "Prohibiting it prevents the natural evolution of the craft and prevents the evolving expression of culture and identity. We should have the option to use it or not."

His current techniques of working silver and gold (both 18-karat and 22-karat) include stampwork, repoussé, lost-wax casting, hammering, planishing, and using a rolling mill to create patterns on the sheet silver he uses—and combinations thereof. "I like to have things have components to them—joints, hinges—make things move, spin, actuate," he says.

For sales he relies upon a handful of retail outlets and three annual retail shows: Santa Fe Indian Market, Heard Museum, and the Eiteljorg Museum. His first show was Indian Market, in 2001. In 2005 he was one of the artists honored with a SWAIA (Southwestern Association for Indian Arts) fellowship.

Of the five years that he has been silversmithing full-time, he says, "It has been tough at times, but I've been so blessed. People were willing to teach me, and each time I need to get some silver I seem to get a sale. Each sale is like a small victory. I am thankful for their buying from me, and really touched and honored that they do so. And especially if they come back."

Cody is the father of three sons and a daughter, and is married to Pilar Agoyo, a fashion designer from San Juan Pueblo.

ELMER SATALA JR.
HOPI

THE YOUNGEST OF FIVE CHILDREN born to Gloria Honanie and Elmer Satala Sr., Elmer was born in 1968 into the Bear Clan. As many did before the Hopi Nation was able to build its own secondary school in 1986, Elmer left Hopi to attend high school. Fortunately he was able to attend Winslow High (from which he graduated in 1988), an hour's drive from his home village of Songoopavi atop Second Mesa. "Then I went off to work in Flagstaff," he says. "I worked at a fast-food restaurant and after eighteen months became the manager. I worked there until I returned home in 1991 for initiation into Wuwutsim," an important religious society.

Elmer went to the famed Hopi Guild to learn how to work silver. Established after World War II to provide silversmithing instruction under the GI Bill, it trained generations of Hopi silversmiths until about 1992, with its mission largely accomplished and most now learning from practicing silversmiths. Elmer was a member of the last graduating class. "There were eighteen in the class when we started, but only seven graduated; part of that was because some left to start out early on their own." As a part of graduation, he says, "They gave you a two-by-six sheet of silver to make a ring, bracelet, a pair of earrings, and pendants. Then there would be a show of that. Your family could pick a piece or two of the jewelry. Then others could buy what was left."

Elmer worked at the Guild from 1992 until 1995. "They would issue materials, and you would turn in the finished work when it was ready." The hardest part? "Coming up with new ideas, something no one else had done yet, and then translating them into silver." While he was at the Guild, Elmer ordered his first hallmark, a simple, straightforward "ES." In 1993 he designed and ordered a new hallmark: a bear paw with a stylized "S" for the pad of the paw.

"In 1996 I tried to go on my own, but I wound up apprenticing with my uncle, Watson Honanie," he says. After Elmer graduated, Honanie, an experienced and well-regarded silver- and goldsmith, had asked Elmer what he wanted to do. "That was when he was telling me about drawing the pieces out and stuff like that. He taught me to high-polish, not satin-finish, from steel wool," the latter being the more common finish for Hopi jewelry since the late 1960s. "He also taught me how important your cutting strategy is, about making sure your designs fit into what you are making. And besides skills, he taught me patience.

"In 2000 I took that knowledge and education and started out on my own. Mostly I was selling to people who had shops up here: Ron McGee, Monongye and Iskasokpu, and Mr. Hawk. Then my girlfriend (Monica Nuvamsa) got a job (in Tucson) in 2002. She was the internship coordinator at the Udall Foundation." In late 2006 they moved back to Hopi, where he continues his silverwork.

Elmer's work has entered a new phase as he experiments with necklaces, articulated pendants, new stones, and gold. But whatever he makes, "I try to put meaning into it, to reflect Hopi life."

RAYNARD SCOTT
NAVAJO

RAYNARD SCOTT WAS BORN IN LOS ANGELES IN 1965 to Louise Nelson and Raymond Scott, who was in Los Angeles to attend business college. They moved back to Fort Defiance and then to Winslow, Arizona, where Ray graduated from Winslow High School in 1983. The oldest of four sons and two daughters, he is the only one who works silver, but that was not the original plan. He learned silver from his folks, who were busily trying to keep up with the demand for work during the boom period of the early to mid 1970s. They produced both overlay and chip inlay, so seven-year-old Ray stepped in, along with the next-oldest son, Ron. First tasks included being general gofers, cleaning up, buffing, and crushing turquoise and mixing epoxy for chip inlay work. As Ray grew older he stayed home to work silver and look after his younger siblings while his folks went on brief road trips to sell work as the overheated boom-period market began to cool. His job then was to do the cutting and sawing, preparation for the soldering his parents would do upon their return.

Following in the footsteps of his father, Ray enrolled at the University of Arizona in the fall of 1983, seeking to earn a bachelor's degree in business with a minor in political science. Jewelry-making was then for him less a way of earning a little extra income than it was a way to get away from the stress of his studies. He recalls making a special-order pin-pendant, a maze design, for a professor. "I charged her $30 for it and immediately called my buddies to meet me at the pizza joint for dinner! Things seemed simpler then and $30

was a good sale. But then recognition of my work and demand for it began growing, and it [silverwork] kind of took over my life," he says.

"My own designs began to develop in the late 1980s—I sublet some studio space in Ganado [Arizona] with another silversmith for a year, 1986 to '87. It was then that I started on the show circuit, where I started selling direct, and I even won a blue ribbon for my work at the Eight Northern Pueblos show in '87. It was confirmation that I had found my calling.

"We even collaborated on a few pieces, and I learned some new techniques and experimented more. I was doing triple overlay and textured backgrounds, I experimented with fusing silver dust for texture, did hammering and stippling with a diamond point ... all kinds of stuff. I got the chance to see the work of White Buffalo, Chuck Supplee, Raymond Yazzie—how their work was so masterfully done, above and beyond the work of others.

"A lot of my ideas are doodling ideas. Some involve an epiphany—architecture is a source of inspiration. I'm influenced by old Greek reliefs, even Gothic. Also, for a while, some Egyptian motifs. My best ideas come when I am so fatigued, when only my mind is working ... about 2 a.m.," he laughs.

Not long after his apprenticeship (with his family) ended, he gained two apprentices himself in Kee Yazzie and Chris Billy, who joined him in 1993. "Both came to the house to my workshop. We worked together for about two or three years, traveling and introducing them to the show circuit and galleries. Everyone shares the same techniques; it is how you apply them that makes the difference."

He first started with gold about 1994, preferring higher-karat gold for its depth, color, and contrast. "I enjoy stones and try and use good ones, but those are few and far between, so my work is more about the metal." His next goal is to learn how to set precious stones.

He now lives in Phoenix, where he settled in 1996 after bouncing back and forth between there and Santa Fe, where his family lived from 1972 to 1983. Santa Fe is still home as well, and Ray tries to spend summers there.

A single dad of three sons and a daughter, he says, "They are all artistic in their own way. No one is picking up silver at this point—they're more into two-dimensional work and sculpture. I don't want to push them as I was pushed."

His hallmark, which he has used since 1984, is Taa'tsohi or Morning Glory, which honors his paternal grandfather, whose name was Hastiin Taa'tsohi.

RAYMOND SEQUAPTEWA
HOPI

RAYMOND WAS BORN AT HOME, in the village of Hotevilla on Third Mesa, in 1948 to Edna (Wishibi) Sequaptewa and Elmer. His Hopi name is Tsoro (Bluebird). Following Hopi tradition, "my dad wove blankets, kilts, belts, and sashes, and Mom wove wicker plaques and made pottery. I would sit down with my dad as he told stories that led into talks about things like the stars, the earth, growing corn, and life. When I wasn't helping my father, I went about on my own, taking walks. I collected all kinds of things along the washes: colored rocks, bits of wood, feathers from birds … things left behind. I visited the places where the petroglyphs were and tried to copy the images. I used to look at the rock and the formations, how they were put together—the layering of rock. I also remember laying in the shade, under a tree, and looking up at the clouds, taking in the shapes and the designs that they would make. I believe that these experiences were my art classes."

He graduated from Phoenix Indian High School in 1967. "I went to trade school for auto mechanics, but when I came back out here to Hopi there was no kind of service station or anything like that, so I wound up in construction. After a project was done I found a job at Wayne Sekaquaptewa's shop [Hopicrafts], cleaning up after the silversmiths went home, hoeing weeds, checking on his livestock—and watching the silversmiths. There were about six or seven silversmiths working there. So after I was done cleaning I would sit down and fiddle around with their scraps and tools. Then one morning I got caught by Wayne, sitting at a table doing stuff, and he asked, would I like to learn? 'Yeah I sure would.' He gave me

an empty bench and basic tools, and the others would help give me hints on making silver. I learned how the metals work, how to cut, solder. I started using plain copper, practicing cutting curves, straight lines, and circles. Copper cuts the same way as silver. Later on Wayne gave me a piece of silver and asked for pendants. He and [his brother] Emory would review my work, pick out a few, and the rest would go back into the scrap bucket. They taught me how to perfect my work. I stayed there with Wayne for about eight years—until he passed away. Then I went to Hopi Arts and Crafts Guild for about seven years until I started getting restless. I had that searching feeling. So, scraping together what I had, I built my own studio at Hotevilla. It was small, but it was my own." By this time he was married to Joy (Sekayumptewa)—a nurse—and they were the parents of three daughters and a son.

"Before I finished it I got really sick. I went to the hospital—everything was going out on me. The doctor gave me a couple years to live. I couldn't produce much—I'd get tired really fast." Thus began a personal journey that would profoundly change his jewelry from conventional Hopi overlay to something whose uniqueness and artistic vision defies description.

"My body was in pain, I had no money, and my shop was not done. I was feeling down, so I would go for long walks on the edge of the mesas. I started picking up small pieces of wood, bones left from animals, and discarded stuff that people had left behind, wondering what I could make from it. One of these walks was a very painful one; I cried that day, and as I was crying I saw something on the ground—a piece of animal bone. It was hollow and when I picked it up and blew into it, it whistled and made a sound like an eagle. I cleaned the bone and took it home. I melted some silver, cast, and mounted it. I saw an old radio at the dump and took it apart. I found an old Hopi moccasin that was sewn together with sinew. The more I looked I could see all these things in these discarded things. The art was already in there: all I had to do was expose them so people could see them. From those treasures I made art pieces to take with me to my first show—the Hopi show in Sedona. Some couldn't understand what I had there. But I sold everything by noon. It was the beginning of my own style, even though at first sight some people laughed at what I had created."

The show gave Raymond the courage and motivation—and the resources—to move forward—"I felt that I was able to breathe." With the proceeds he purchased silver and other materials for his work.

Others have had an influence on his work, some in unexpected circumstances. "One day as I was working at my studio I saw a *bahana* (white man) walking down the road with a walking stick. He seemed a little lost and looked out of place." Raymond greeted him and gave him some apricots from his tiny orchard. Noon found Raymond on his way past Orayvi, where he saw the same man and invited him to go eat with him. "There was something about this man and I felt I could trust him. My studio was empty and I told him that he could stay there for a few days if he wanted. I had scraps and materials lying around and he asked me if he could use some. The man turned out to be a gifted artist in his own right and "in his short stay taught me how to really see the materials that I used … what's in the rock formations, the texture, lighting, the grains that run through wood. I started working more creatively and things seemed to fall in place naturally. Years later I became friends with another artist, Paul Kretzman, and he showed me about etching, engraving, and about metals. He taught me about modern art, European art, and contemporary art forms."

These new ideas and techniques were filtered through his own experiences and background, and adapted to his own artistic vision. "I picked and chose what I wanted to use, keeping in mind who I was, where I came from, and my culture. I didn't want to uproot myself."

Then illness changed his life again. "This time it was my kidneys." Despite dialysis treatments "I knew I didn't have long to live. I started thinking about my life and what was beyond that, about how can I leave a piece of myself behind? I put a lot of my thoughts into my pieces at that time."

After four years, with the insistence of his family, he agreed to have one of his daughters give him a kidney. "I gave her life and now she gave me my life." Three years later he needed a triple bypass. "This would be my ultimate test of my will to live. It has been two years since then and I am still here. I wanted to live and was not ready to leave this place."

He observes that after such an experience "you become more aware of what's around you. I wanted my art pieces to reflect that. I made them more alive, adding more color and adding other things that brought them alive. I started speaking to my pieces saying, 'Okay now, whatever you turn out to be, I'll work with you and let you create yourself.'"

And so, this remarkable man continues on a personal journey, whose difficulties have only strengthened him. He has responded to the challenges and heartbreak not with anger but with art—and thereby enriched the lives of others.

HOWARD AND PATRICIA SICE
LAGUNA (HOWARD)
AND NAVAJO (PATRICIA)

HOWARD SICE, A LAGUNA-HOPI, was born to James Sice and Edith Satala in Winslow, Arizona, in 1948 but was raised at the Laguna village of Paraje as a member of the Corn Clan. Howard's parents, his brother James, and his sister are career professionals, a path Howard also started out on after attending St. Michaels High School on the Navajo Reservation and graduating from Winslow High in 1967. He entered Northern Arizona University but found himself the proverbial starving student; his scholarship covered tuition, books, and food, but not on weekends. It was then that he received a letter from the Army and immediately headed over to see the Air Force recruiter, "who said he could swear me in tomorrow," Howard says. "I told my folks I was going to see Europe. I never did," he laughs, "but I did see Johnson, Wake, and Midway Islands along with the New Hebrides, Vietnam, Australia, and Hawaii."

In 1970 he married Patricia Smith (born in Ganado, Arizona, in 1949), whom he had met when they both attended high school at St. Michaels. Her father and mother (Howard and Nellie Smith) made jewelry, as did her grandfather. Her brothers, Patrick and Edison, are accomplished jewelry artists who have won acclaim for their work, Patrick creating contemporary inlay work and Edison creating his interpretation of traditional older jewelry, inspired by the work of his father, who is also a *hataałi* (medicine man; literally, "a singer"). The elder Smiths lived near Steamboat, Arizona, selling their work locally, for the most part, until Edison came home and started working silver and selling it to buyers from Phoenix, Tucson, Albuquerque, and Santa Fe.

Their marriage occurred while Howard was on leave in Flagstaff, after his return from thirteen months in Vietnam as a field medic. Upon his return he was assigned to aerospace medical research labs at Wright-Patterson Air Force Base in Ohio. An interesting background for someone known now for his jewelry, but perhaps a partial explanation of his unusual approach to jewelry-making and his willingness to experiment.

"I started jewelry because I married into a jewelry-making family," he laughs. "On our way to Wright Patterson AFB in Ohio we stopped off in Flagstaff to visit Patricia's folks. My father-in-law gave me some silver, turquoise, and coral and said, 'Get to work.'" It was, of course, a little more than that, as Pat's father showed him how to solder and set stones, but that was about it. "I'm pretty much self-taught. I did a lot of repairs while in Ohio—learning techniques from other artists and studying their work as a part of repairing. I repaired pieces by Gibson Nez, Quandelacy, a Loloma piece—all these big names I had seen in *Arizona Highways* magazine and admired. Repairing them gave me the chance to study the pieces." While there he also had the opportunity to admire and study the engraving work done by a Vandalia, Ohio, gunsmith.

But Howard is not one to copy the work of others, no matter how successful. He was reassigned to Davis-Monthan Air Force Base in Tucson, Arizona, in 1981. By 1982 he had started engraving work, following up on the interest first sparked in Ohio. "I chose engraving for my work because there was no one doing it," he explains. "Patricia started helping right at the beginning and is instrumental in quality control and some in design. Also, I brainstorm with her. We set up a booth at the San Xavier Wa:k [festival], and while we were there Pat saw a small silver bowl, set with a single turquoise, that was selling for $80. She said, 'You should try something like that.'" And he did. He still has that first bowl, which is dwarfed by later creations that measure up to a foot across.

The history of their jewelry-making is one of experimentation and innovation. They started using exotic metals like titanium and niobium around 1985. These are heat-resistant, so they cannot be soldered; any fastening has to be done by riveting the metals. "I learned how to work with them from Bill Seely in Jerome [Arizona]," Howard says. "I bought equipment and materials. The basic instruction took about twenty minutes. The technique is easy but very exacting." Other metals he has worked with include Japanese alloys such as shaku do, mokume gane, and shibu ichi. Always seeking new materials to enhance or inspire their designs, the Sices have also worked with a range of faceted gemstones and minerals, including peridot, amethyst, sapphires, tourmalines, and moldavite.

In 1990 Howard received a commission from the Phoenix Commission on the Arts that was part of the very first percent-for-the-arts project in Arizona: to beautify Central Avenue in downtown Phoenix. For submissions, he says, "I did six drawings. Life-size, butcher paper. Forty-two inches across. They liked the idea but not all the drawings, so I made six more. They took four from the first and two from the second batch."

"The designs were all petroglyphs from Arizona except for one with people that was Howard's work," explains Pat, "and that one became the symbol for the whole project." Combining the various elements in different ways, Howard created 100 unique medallions that are seen by thousands of motorists every day.

Pat and Howard's children have learned silverwork but are pursuing other interests as well. Their son, Robert, in addition to winning prizes at SWAIA for his jewelry creations while still in high school, is drawn to composing music. Daughter Adrienne makes jewelry and, along with her dad, engraves earrings and makes handmade sterling chains.

In 1992 Howard was awarded a SWAIA fellowship, which allowed him to remodel a room in his home to use as a workshop and to purchase more materials. They have since moved to his home village of Laguna and then back to Tucson. There the music he listens to each day (techno at the moment) is a source of inspiration as he and Pat thoughtfully and meticulously design and create jewelry and follow their motto for Sice Design: "Surprise the senses, challenge the normal, and change the future."

ROGER SKEET JR.
NAVAJO

"I WOULD LIKE TO HAVE GONE TO SCHOOL and served my people on the tribal council," he says, but things turned out differently for Roger Skeet. He was born to the 'Áshiihí (Salt) and Dibé łizhiní (Black Sheep) Clans and for the Kin yaa'áanii (Towering House) Clan in 1933. The oldest of Hanesbah and Roger Skeet Sr.'s eight children, Roger was tapped by his father to stay home and help while all the others went to school. At age eighteen he did try school but left after two months, though not before being taught his ABCs by the Rehoboth missionaries across the road. His upbringing also meant he never became fluent in English, so the initial interview and the follow-up were conducted in Navajo with the help of his daughter, Geraldine, and my other half, Emmi.

His apprenticeship began at age eight, learning each skill, each aspect, each technique of silverworking one step at a time. And the hardest thing to learn? A moment to think and a smile breaks across his face as he remembers: soldering. It is a skill that is most often mentioned by silversmiths as the trickiest to learn to do properly.

Roger Sr. began working silver in an era when a number of smiths were still using silver ingots. The ingots he and his father, Chahi Begay (who like Roger had been born in Pinehaven, New Mexico), used into the 1950s were the round kind, reminiscent of the silver coinage, American and Mexican, that had been used by Navajo silversmiths since they first started working silver in the 1860s. "They came in a little pouch," he recalls. "We would pound silver first and then roll it to make sheet." While Roger Sr. and Jr. are best

166 SILVER & STONE

known for their fine stampwork and file-and-chisel work, they were versatile jewelry artists. "We used to occasionally do sand-cast work—for nazhas [also spelled najas], rings, buckles, and ketohs. I haven't done that since 1967."

Roger and his dad also made the silver frames for bracelets for C. G. Wallace, who had Zuni artists inlay them with turquoise. Fashioning the frames was not Roger's favorite type of jewelry-making, and he has not done that style of work since his father died. The last piece they made together with a silver frame on it was a concha belt that was later inlaid with turquoise by a Zuni lapidarist.

While Roger continued working with his father, making concha belts, squash-blossom necklaces, horse bridles, buckles, bracelets, and guard bracelets of heavy triangle, half-round, round, and square wire, he also worked on his own, making items for the Navajo Guild in Window Rock, Arizona, as did his father. Roger Jr. began using the hallmark "R.S." about 1955 "when they [the Navajo Guild] started requiring it." He had a hallmark made for him that read "ROGER SKEET JR," but the metal proved to be brittle and soon broke, so Roger went back to "R.S." and "RS."

After his father died in 1959, Roger Jr. began making his own jewelry and designs, though he also continued to make many of the kinds of pieces he and his father had worked on in the years before, using many of the tools he inherited from him. Their work is indistinguishable to everyone but Roger Jr., who can detect the tiny differences in stampwork tools that tell him which is his and which is his father's. Asked about his father's work, Roger quickly brings out a copy of an old auction catalog of the C. G. Wallace collection. Roger turns to two well-worn pages, pointing out work that was misidentified, notably a belt made by his father in 1940 that was inlaid by Zuni artist Lambert Homer but was attributed to Roger Jr. and dated 1936 … when Roger would have been three years old.

Asked whose work he admires, Roger cites Ambrose Roanhorse, from Fort Wingate, New Mexico. Roanhorse and Ambrose Lincoln (who are often confused with one another) and the Skeets made similar-style concha belts, which led to competition between the smiths as well as confusion of their work by dealers and collectors. Here again, Roger can readily discern the differences in their work.

Now in his seventies, Roger says he is retiring, which for him means scaling back and no longer taking orders as much as simply producing what he wants, when he wants. You are most likely to find him working around the family home, hauling firewood, feeding his animals and hauling water for them—and occasionally making a concha belt.

JASON TAKALA SR.
HOPI

JASON TAKALA OF SONGOOPAVI VILLAGE WAS BORN IN 1955, one of ten children, to Jackson Takala and Della Dawahoya. At the time of the interview, his mother, age eighty-three, was still living and still weaving baskets. Jason married Margie Lomayaktewa in 1977; they have five children: Jaylene Histia, Jayme Nuvalawu, Marcie, Jason Jr., and Mina.

Jason Sr. began learning silverwork at sixteen. He had just gotten out of summer school in Woodstock, Vermont, a school he had been able to attend through the Dartmouth A Better Chance (ABC) program, for which a counselor at Phoenix Indian School had encouraged him to apply shortly after his freshman year. An entrance exam must be passed in order to qualify for the Dartmouth-run summer program, in which participants take freshman-level college classes.

"I used to design for my uncle [Bernard Dawahoya] during summers," he says. "I would watch the workers who used to work for him. Then I decided to try it out myself, so I went to the Hopi Guild shop … without knowing how to cut or anything," he laughs. "I pretty much taught myself."

In 1977 Jason and Margie moved to Phoenix, where Jason could more easily make a living at silversmithing. While there, he worked with the well-known jeweler Pierre Touraine, who has mentored a number of American Indian jewelry artists. "What he put in my head was: the most important thing in jewelry was designing. He also taught me how to meticulously clean my jewelry, which is important for a good final appearance. I worked with him

for five years. Charles Supplee [a Hopi] was there then, too. I would take a stone to him, and he would work with me how to design around the stone to catch the eye."

They left Phoenix about 1987, returning to Hopi for a decade before settling in Holbrook in 1997. "Moving back to Hopi was a difficult thing to do, but my work was revolving only around the man-in-the-maze design," he says. "I needed to create, to let my artistic ability take over. Only place I could do this was back on Hopi. I am also from the old school, where you are taught or lectured by your uncles; you have to show them that you can listen to them and learn the lessons. I came back to Hopi to build a home for my family. This is the most important thing a man has to do. We [later] chose to live in Holbrook for its school and because it is only an hour or so drive to home, to Hopi. It is also a place my customers cannot miss, going east or west … and it's a small community, with no Wal-Mart!"

While many who work silver say soldering is the most difficult skill to master, Jason finds that designing is the hardest part, "because you always have to be one step ahead of anybody else—the copiers."

Jason is not likely to ever have trouble with copies where his maze jewelry is concerned. He started cutting mazes in the mid-1980s, just before Hopi silversmith Glenn Lucas (who was much admired and well-liked among the community of other silversmiths) died. "It was kind of a gift he gave to me, because when his health was deteriorating I kind of picked it up," Jason says. "It was something that just came to me. My first maze was a buckle, which I took to the Heard Museum. They sold it the same day. Byron [Hunter, then manager of the museum shop] ordered six more."

Jason's cutting skills were truly tested, if not honed, when sheet silver hit $60 an ounce. "I had to make an adjustment on my creativity, so I started making stud earrings that were 1/8 inch in diameter. Bear paws, flute players, hummingbirds—you name it—was on those little post earrings. That's where my intricate cutting came from." The first small complete maze came about 1997 or so. "I cut both ways, from both directions, using 0000 blades only. I start a cut on the outside going in and then start a cut on the inside going out. You have to be extremely careful with forward pressure." Knowing how he does it is no shortcut to duplicating the intricate, tiny mazes he creates, mazes so finely cut that no one else has successfully attempted it since he started. "I am well known for the maze, so most everything I do has to have the maze in it. I tried running away from it, but …"

All of his designs are executed freehand, starting only with width measurements for the overall piece. Unlike many smiths, he uses silver solder when working on a gold-on-silver piece of jewelry—"the first order I had for that was from you [Bahti Indian Arts], sometime in the mid-1980s." He prefers that to gold-on-gold (also begun in the mid-1980s), "which gets real tricky. The first gold-on-gold order came from Richard Mehagian of Kopavi, in Sedona."

He sells most of his work wholesale, selling direct only at the Heard Museum in March, in Estes Park in July, and at the Santa Fe Indian Market in August. His work now is given a high polish on a cloth buffing wheel rather than the matte finish with 0000 steel wool that Hopi jewelry was once known for. He attributes the change to the market rather than his own preference.

His orders come in steadily from across the country and, since the mid-1990s, from Japan, where orders since about 2000 have been more for his work set with stones.

Asked what he would be doing if he were not a silversmith, he replies after a moment, "Probably I'd be a high school counselor." This aspiration reflects his commitment to family and the Hopi value of helping others in the community.

JACK AND MARY TOM
NAVAJO

JACK WAS BORN to the 'Áshiihí (Salt) Clan and for the Tó dích'íi'nii (Bitterwater) Clan in 1948 at Keams Canyon, Arizona, to Sadie and Jim Tom. His father, a bricklayer and a coal miner, was also a hataałi who knew the Shooting Way, a healing ritual used to cure a range of illnesses associated with lightning, from paralysis to nervousness. Jack was struck by lightning in 1979 while working for the railroad. His employer laid him off and so, jobless and injured, he returned home to his father, who performed the Shooting Way ceremony to restore his son to *hozhon*—health and harmony.

Having been through the experience, he feels safe in incorporating lightning motifs in his work. His work also employs Hopi motifs, something he attributes to the fact that his great-grandmother was Hopi. "It's why I do some of my designs in Hopi style," he says. He finds designing to be the challenging part of silversmithing, "trying to create something different," but adds, "I like trying different stuff." But Jack does not work his designs out on paper: "I don't draw. I start a piece of it and it goes that way. … I draw it in my head and then draw it in silver. Sometimes it takes a while because you have got to think how you are going to put it together." His work also incorporates Navajo rug designs as well as ancient Anasazi patterns. Jack notes, "They taught me that the old ones left it [the designs] for others to use, for us to use."

One of six children, Jack attended Intermountain School in Utah, graduating in 1968, but it was not until 1971 that he began working jewelry. That was also the year he married

Mary Begay. Mary was born to the Tóbaahí (Water's Edge) Clan and for the Tsi'naajinii (Black-Streaked Wood) Clan in 1949 to Joe Begay and Mary Dixon. Her father worked on the railroad in Santa Cruz, California. Of the eight siblings, only Mary and her brother Steven Begay are silversmiths. (Steven makes stampwork jewelry.) Mary started out fabricating the silver and the silver-and-gold beads that grace the pendants and necklaces she makes with Jack. In addition to the work she and Jack create together, Mary now designs and creates very clean, contemporary pendants and necklaces of her own, frequently set with spiny oyster shell. At shows, Jack's beautiful inlay work and Mary's unique pieces are entered individually, but work they have made together is frequently entered under one name (usually Jack's), as most shows do not allow work to be entered unless the artist has

purchased a booth and a few charge an extra fee for a second artist—even if they are husband and wife.

Jack and Mary are parents of four children and a niece they raised since age one—"I count her as my daughter," says Mary. The youngest, Lucas, is still in high school and competed in basketball in the 2006 Indigenous Games in Colorado. Another child, Michelle, has entered medical school; eldest son Rufus, married with two children, works as a carpenter; and niece Dawndee works for the Indian Health Service. Only their oldest child, Angie Tom, a mother of two, makes jewelry, having started about five years ago, when she was twenty-nine.

Jack began his career by working for a jewelry shop in Holbrook, Arizona, starting as the boom period was about to begin. Working as a buffer, he found it an unpleasant and dirty job, but it did provide Jack with the opportunity to observe silversmithing and, ultimately, teach himself the craft.

In 1979, after silver prices shot up, the cost of silver forced him, like many silversmiths, out of the profession. He left Holbrook and silversmithing to return to work on the railroad and then to train as a welder in Phoenix. He spent four years as a welder before returning to silvermaking in 1985.

The first show the couple entered was the 1974 Holbrook Navajo County Fair, where their work won three ribbons. At that time their work was more traditional, set with turquoise. Jack modestly attributes the success of his early items to using "nice stones (turquoise)—you don't find those anymore: really good Lone Mountain spiderweb, Bisbee …" Coral is the stone they most like to work with now, but they also search for fine opals and buy and trade for the best turquoise they can locate, saving the finest stones for pieces made for shows and competitions. About 1994 they further enhanced their work with the use of 14-karat gold.

In the years since that first competition Jack has won ribbons from all the major Indian arts shows, including the Heard Museum, Santa Fe Indian Market, Museum of Northern Arizona, and Eight Northern Pueblos.

Their metalworking techniques have expanded to include textured rolling (which Jack learned from Zuni jeweler Marvin Panteah) and sandblasting, which provides an alternative to the normal mirror-finish polish most silversmiths give to the back of their work. The changes are part of the process that allows their work to continue to evolve and enchant.

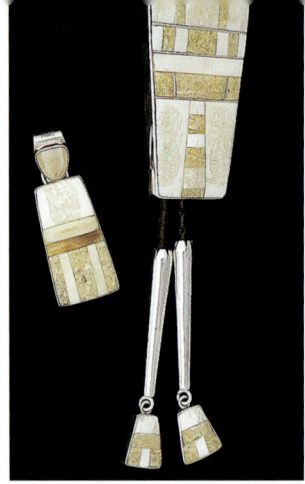

ROGER TSABETSAYE SR.
ZUNI

BORN IN 1941, ROGER TSABETSAYE SR. (whose Zuni name is Iyahokque, or Early Flower) belongs to the Mustard Clan, as did La:niyahdi, the first Zuni to work silver. His parents were Susana Gaspar and Joe Tsabetsaye Sr. of the Eagle Clan. Young Roger was nicknamed Atsa'bee atsay, Eagle Tail, from his habit of tailing his father around everywhere. He was the sixth of eight children, the others being Jane, Mary, Joe Jr., Caroline, Edith, Cecelia, and Joanita. He and Edith, famed for her needlepoint jewelry, are the only two who pursued careers in jewelry-making. Joe Sr. (b. 1914) made cluster jewelry and was a jack-of-all-trades, most notably a jockey at the heavily attended horse races held regularly at Gamerco, New Mexico, just north of Gallup. He was easy to spot as he always raced wearing traditional Zuni clothes, frequently winning.

Roger attended school in Zuni at St. Anthony's through the eighth grade and then went to the Albuquerque Indian School, far from home, graduating in 1960. It was not unusual for students, especially first-year students, to suffer painful homesickness. "Some of my [Zuni] schoolmates ran home," Roger says. "It took them a week.

"I tried to volunteer for military right out of high school, but I had back problems and eyesight problems. I tried several times but they wouldn't take me—not even the Forest Service." So instead he transferred to the Santa Fe Indian School (1960–61) just before it became the famed Institute of American Indian Art. The well-known and well-regarded artist and educator Geronima Montoya was his teacher there. "I remember I got in trouble with her one time—I was always in trouble," he laughs. "We were supposed to do a two-dimensional piece for the school to enter in the annual Scottsdale National Indian Art Show. I did another in my room that was all cubic and symbolic. I had a vision about our creation story, about life, about birth. I called it 'Returning Home.' I didn't want to do it in a real way, only in abstract. I sent it to the Scottsdale Indian Art Show, paying for it out of my own pocket. Well, she got a phone call about my work winning a major prize [Student with the Greatest Promise]. When she learned it wasn't the piece I did for the class but an abstract piece—the one I entered on my own—she wasn't too happy, but she couldn't say anything.

"When I got out of high school there was a talent search for students to attend the Southwest Indian Art Project [SWIAP] at the University of Arizona, down in Tucson. Joe Herrera, Charles and Otellie Loloma, and others were going to be the teachers. I was accepted and started the following summer. I spent a total of three summers at the U of A. There was a lot of turnover among the students, but the ones I remember include Manfred Susunkewa from Hopi, Frank Austin, Antoine Warrior, Jim Redcorn, Terrance Talaswaima, Helen Hardin, Barton Ghahate, Anderson Lessansee, Ernest Whitehead from San Carlos Apache … We had a pretty good time, and we all pretty much stuck together there.

"The first year in the program I was taking jewelry-making. Charles [Loloma] chased me out of his class, because coming from Zuni I knew some lapidary, and he thought I insulted him because I said that isn't the way to cut stone. He was also teaching lost-wax and tufa-cast.

"Then [at IAIA] I got into textiles, with Lloyd New. He had graduated from the Chicago Art Institute and wanted me, after the first year, to go there, too. I applied but only my tuition was paid; there was no money available for housing and other expenses, so I couldn't attend. I wound up attending the Rochester Institute of Technology School of American Craftsmen 1963 to 65 in New York, with scholarship money that was left over from SWIAP. I really enjoyed it, studying silversmithing, mostly planished work. When I got back from New York I had a new hallmark stamp made: an eagle fan with talons.

"I went into business for myself, starting Tsabetsaye Enterprises. I started a little market in 1970—a convenience store with arts and crafts. I ran it until 1985." Almost from the beginning, Roger's silverwork brought him attention and fame. President Johnson gave one of Roger's silver necklaces to Queen Juliana of the Netherlands, and examples of his jewelry are in the Smithsonian and represented in the collections of the finest examples of American Indian jewelry from the latter half of the twentieth century.

Roger has six children: Carmen and Roger Jr. (of Zuni–Zia heritage), and Darryl, Roderick, Johnna, and Renee (of Zuni heritage). Carmen is the one following her father into the arts. Her focus, however, is filmmaking. Roger, far from being retired, continues to fashion distinctive jewelry that reflects his position as one of the early innovators in American Indian jewelry—artists who helped dismantle the barriers that had confined American Indian artists to non-Indian notions of what their art was supposed to be.

ORVILLE TSINNIE
NAVAJO

SAYS ORVILLE TSINNIE, "My grandfather used to tell me that when Creator sends you a gift in the way of turquoise, don't send it away or Creator will be offended."

Many paths have led people to careers as silversmiths; for Orville Tsinnie the path began with a career in law enforcement. He attended Tuba City High School through his sophomore year, "and then I moved to Chinle [Arizona], where I had a favorite uncle working for the Bureau of Indian Affairs," he recalls. "That's where I graduated—I took correspondence courses and graduated end of my junior year. Thereafter I went to the Haskell Institute [in Lawrence, Kansas], studying commercial business, but I didn't finish. Instead I came back and landed a job with the Navajo Police Department. I liked it, enjoyed the work, even though we usually worked a twelve-hour day and were paid for eight—the rest were 'volunteered.' One day shortly before the shift ended, about 8 p.m., a sergeant and I were ordered to witness an autopsy of a body that had been missing for a few weeks, found out near Hardrock. That was quite an experience. Three hours later I was thoroughly messed up. The mortician was whistling along, flipping things out [of the body]. Finally he locates cause of death [strangulation]. I was wearing a triple-filter mask … but oooh. I got back home, went inside the front door and took my uniform off and tried to scrub myself off. No good. I didn't sleep well. Next day I put on regular clothes, turned in my weapon and uniform, and that was that."

And "that" sent him to a job delivering commodity foods, work with a job-development program, a position as assistant director of personnel for the Navajo Nation, and, finally, silversmithing.

Orville was born in Tuba City in 1943; his father was a maintenance man, and young Orville had access to his welding machine, giving him his first exposure to working metal. "In the summertime I had all the time in the world to tag along with my dad," he says. "And my older brother was a really good welder, so I learned a lot from him, too."

When he married his wife, Darlene, he was working in Window Rock. "When we were there my sister and her husband, who was a Hopi jeweler, urged me to register at the Navajo Community College in Many Farms, Arizona, so I could learn silver," he says. "But I resisted: I had a job, a good job. But my wife couldn't get used to Window Rock and wanted to move back [to Shiprock]. My mom's mom was from nearby Sanostee, and I had relatives [in Shiprock] so it wasn't that big a deal for me to move here. So one day in 1972, I put on a suit and tie for the last time and moved here jobless and into low-rent housing. That was Thursday. On Sunday a white guy was knocking on my door and offered me a job to oversee the Navajo Engineering and Construction Authority [NECA] heavy-equipment training center and help the new general manager. Well, my wife's grandmother Ann Yellowstone lived nearby. She had gone to a BIA school and had learned silverworking. I got acquainted with her family and spent a lot of time with them when they were working silver. I would just watch. I had no intentions of becoming a jeweler: I had a job—I was set. But then as the years went by things changed. Kind of suddenly," he smiles.

The day after their oldest daughter (Ardiss, now an R.N.) was born, his sister (also a jeweler) was urging him to try something. Laughing again, he recalls, "She threw me a piece of copper and told me to make something and I said, 'Seems to me if you wanted me to be a silversmith you'd give me a piece of silver.'" And so she gave him a piece of 18-gauge silver, about two-by-three inches. "The first thing that came to my mind was overlay because he [the brother-in-law] was doing overlay. I scribed out a Navajo girl [based on a paper doll] and inlaid it. After that you could say I was on fire. I ended up making three rings that day. The pin we still have.

"After the day was over my sister suggested I start with making rings and made a list of tools and silver supplies I would need. My income-tax refund was there in the mail, so I paid the hospital delivery bill and still had money left over. I went to Tohtah Silver in west Farmington, run by the Weaver brothers. I bought a compass, rulers, silver, stones, torch … spent three-hundred-and-some-odd dollars of our income-tax check on supplies and set up shop in the corner of one of the back rooms. It wasn't as easy as doing it with my sister and brother-in-law there to help. It was all trial-and-error and lots of error, but three weeks later I had the hang of it. It's all a matter of being able to work the metal the way you want, and my welding experience helped." He left NECA that year, 1973, to embark on his new career as a silversmith, and never looked back.

"Several times I went to the Four Corners Monument to sell and I went to people like Bob French, Russell Foutz, and Aztec Ruins Trading Post and Sue and Russell Adams," he says. "All of the traders took to me well—they saw something I didn't see at the time. They would critique my jewelry but reward me for that hurt by buying some … They urged an older style. Said their customers wanted 'old style' work. They would let me go into their walk-in vaults where I could see old stuff they had. Sue told me, 'Don't copy—take a mouthful of what we show you but evolve.' She taught me a lot. Bob [French, of Waterflow Trading] used to reward me just by buying. One thing Bob and Sue never did, was never look at the price on the bottom—they just looked at the work. As I got better the work sold better."

It didn't hurt that he began his silversmithing career as the boom period hit. Soon after he started working silver at home full-time, he was invited to do home shows in Arizona

and California. His first home show, six weeks after he began his new career, was arranged through a younger sister. It was in tiny Page, Arizona, on the shores of Lake Powell. It netted $3,600 in sales.

He started using a hallmark based upon his family's livestock brand, OZT (arranged vertically), but settled on his last name, in block letters. "Then almost within the same year I decided to go with 'Orville and Darlene,'" he says. "Then about 1980 I began to use 'Orville Tsinnie of New Mexico' with two little Shiprocks. I still have that hallmark and use that on certain things that are smaller. On larger pieces I use 'Orville Tsinnie. Shiprock, New Mexico.' And on most belts I stamp every concha. Early on I was making a lot of conchas. Conchas, conchas … I concha'd out, but it was just in time, when their popularity fell off."

Reflecting, he observes that "I started to get full of myself and let so much go by before I realized what I had." But this is clearly a man who now knows what he has, and whose

feet are firmly planted on the ground. And he has a reputation among many silversmiths as someone ready to help with advice on everything from technique to marketing to pricing. And with his keen eye he appreciates the work of others. "I admire quite a number," he says. "The late Andy Kirk, Jake Livingston, Edison Cummings—he is a kid that is *sooo* good he doesn't know what he has—and Julian Lovato."

Orville is an interesting man, by turns serious, humorous, and philosophical. He is, like most Navajos today, caught in an era of great change with concerns about how Navajo culture is changing, how to be successful in the twenty-first century, what it means to be Navajo in the twenty-first century, and questions about the importance of the Navajo language and its chances for survival by the end of the twenty-first century. "Two of my girls graduated from ASU and came back to reverse culture shock. I had never encouraged them to speak Navajo. *I* didn't learn Navajo until I was a sophomore in high school. I wound up on a summer work project with adult Navajos—mostly clan relatives—and the foreman didn't show up. So all of a sudden I am foreman at age sixteen because the real foreman didn't show up and I could read the English job description, but I needed to communicate that in Navajo. We did four or five projects that summer and in the process I finally learned to speak Navajo."

All five of his daughters have gone to college. One, Darlys, "has the talent to build jewelry. The first few pieces she made sold right away, and for a good price. She is a natural and has the personality and touch for it, but I wanted her to go to school. I've done well with the education that I've got, and I know the importance of pursuing what you want."

ED AND JENNIE VICENTI
ZUNI

BOTH EDISON (B. 1945) and Jennie (b. 1944) were born and raised in Zuni Pueblo and now live in Zuni in a home they built, but in between their careers took them far afield. However, even while living many hundreds of miles away, they found the time and need to return to Zuni for important religious events, and they continued a tradition of silverwork they had each learned as children.

Ed, a genial gentleman in every sense of the word, was one of six sons and six daughters born to Celesita Yawakia and Cecil Vicenti. He is the only one of the twelve children currently working silver. "My dad was pretty much a farmer and rancher, and my mom made jewelry in her early years—for groceries and things like that," he recalls. "Mostly she made little squash-blossom necklaces, bracelet rings, in cluster and petit-point style. In her later years she started making pottery. But I didn't really learn silverwork from her—I used to help my dad with the sheep on the ranch." Silversmithing is a family tradition that reaches back to his maternal grandparents' clan uncle, La:niyahdi, the first Zuni to work silver, and Ed would eventually find that the tradition would reach into the future to tap him as a new member.

Jennie is the daughter of Anita Besselente and Buddy Hattie. Her brother, Derrick Hattie, did some inlay work at one time, and Josie Owaleon, one of her two sisters, makes jewelry. Both parents silversmithed full-time, entering their cluster and petit-point work in the Gallup Intertribal Ceremonial, where it frequently garnered prize

ribbons. "That's where I learned, from them," she says. "My dad was the one who taught us kids. He was my mentor. He surprised us with his extra tools so we could start working on our own jewelry."

Recounts Ed: "After we got married we were living in Sacaton [Arizona], where Jennie worked at Phoenix Indian Hospital after she finished nursing school. I had been a student at New Mexico Highlands [University] and was working on my degree in electronics; my high school advanced math and science teacher had encouraged me in that direction." Ed earned his BA in 1968 and was promptly hired by IBM, with whom he had a distinguished career for the next twenty-eight years.

Early on they created a jewelry-making style that played to their mutual strengths, with Ed doing the stonecutting and Jennie doing the silver (since then their roles have reversed). "At Sacaton we started with petit-point, then we got into needlepoint," explains Jennie. "My parents were doing petit-point, in kind of a flat style. We wanted to do our own style. By accident Ed came up with a different stone cut, more domed and pointed down at each end and pretty long."

The job with IBM meant a move to the company's facility in Boulder, Colorado. Living in nearby Longmont, they continued to make jewelry. Says Jennie, "We used to do a lot of shows in Boulder, and in Denver at the Merchandise Mart. We were doing a lot of retailing at shows then; we also wholesaled to Jane Bowman and the Kohlberg store in Denver and became very good friends with the Kohlbergs."

Jennie was making jewelry full-time, having quit nursing once Ed received his BA and she had their first child. (They have two daughters and two sons.) Ed focused on his career: "I worked hard, as I was an engineer-designer in product development, starting with the tape drive … we had tight schedules we had to meet. I worked overtime a lot."

His two sons have followed in his footsteps, with careers in fiber-optic and network-system installation.

But through it all they continued creating jewelry. "She did the work and designing," says Ed. "She would make the prototype, and I made the copies. I wasn't that good at design, so she was the one who designed new pieces." The big change came in 1979 when they were moved to IBM's new location in Tucson.

"That was a big influence on our work," says Ed. "There was the gem show [the annual, monstrous Tucson Gem, Mineral, and Fossil Show] and the Tucson Lapidary Club that we both joined. Jennie got involved in faceting gems, and we learned inlay work. We had been buying turquoise from an old rock shop in Scottsdale, but at the gem show we saw material from all over the world and bought and tried a lot of material, like prystine. We bought a couple of kilos of coral from Italy that we stored away. A good thing we did that," he smiles. The price of coral has soared over the past two decades as its availability has plummeted. Jennie started using gemstones she faceted herself in 1980, about the same time she also began doing inlay work.

Then in 1998 Ed retired from IBM and they returned to Zuni. He may have retired as an electrical engineer-designer, but he did not retire from silversmithing. They work together now, creating pieces that reflect the varied stonecutting and metalworking techniques they have learned and mastered, and using a range of materials: coral, lapis, sugilite, and many types of turquoise. They also use more gold, which they started with about 1990. No longer having to commute back and forth, they are truly home, the place that nurtured the jewelry-making tradition they are a part of, a tradition that they continue and a tradition that they enrich with their own artistic vision and skills.

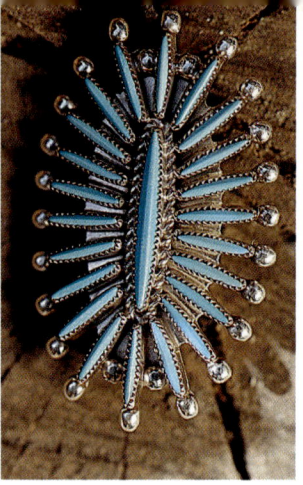

BRYANT WAATSA SR.
ZUNI

BORN INTO THE CROW CLAN AT ZUNI IN 1918, Bryant was one of two sons and two daughters. His mother, Lutie Tsanuti, did not make jewelry, but his father did. "In the olden days we don't work like we do now," Bryant says. "No fancy designs, just basically round [turquoise] sets."

His father did both rows and cluster-style work and, like most silversmiths of his day, made his own wire and sheet. "Dad rolled sheet and used a draw plate for wire. Made his own solder using silver and brass from an old brass washboard he cut up. He bought silver in square ingots that he rolled out." Bryant grimaces wryly, recalling how soldering was the hardest skill to master. "Sometimes it seems like a bezel just wouldn't want to stick and then you kind of have to tear it off and replace it."

Bryant learned how to work silver and cut turquoise from his father. Bryant might have made silver part-time while going to school, but then "My dad died when I was about fifteen years old [a year after he began to teach Bryant jewelry-making]. I had to take over the bills. It was really hard to get a job back then [during the Great Depression], so I had to take over making jewelry." The first piece of jewelry he made was in the style of his father: a bracelet set with a row of round-cut turquoise.

Bryant sold to all the old-time Zuni traders, including Ed Kelsey, the Vanderwagens, and C. G. Wallace. He worked mostly on a special-order basis, as it was easier to sell work that way. Bryant furnished his own turquoise and silver when filling the orders. Even

though it might mean buying the materials on credit, it gave him a little more independence, not having to weigh out materials and weigh them back in, a system that some jewelers find onerous.

Not having the kind of equipment that is available today, especially lapidary trim saws, they used to snip the turquoise into pieces approximately the right width and length, but "it wastes a lot of turquoise that way," says Bryant. "We used to not have any electricity, just gas lamps at night and gasoline torches." For grinding and polishing they used hand-cranked grinders and polishers. Asked if someone cranked while the other ground and polished the turquoise, Bryant shakes his head and pantomimes the motion as he explains that you cranked with one hand and held the stone with the other. Looking at the delicate stonework, one quickly realizes the practice and skill that went into making jewelry before World War II.

While he started out making single- and double-row round-cut turquoise rings and bracelets like his father, Bryant was an innovator. He pioneered needlepoint work in the late 1930s: "It was a few years before the war I started making needlepoint jewelry. I'm the original one." His earliest pieces had the tiny silver drops set to the inside, between the knife-like bezels. After World War II he began to set them to the outside edge.

"I was in the Army during the war," he says. "In 1945 they sent me to Clark Field in the Philippines. I had started out in infantry, but then they gave me engineer training. After the war in the Pacific was over, they found I had three kids, and when they found that out they sent me home." During the war, before and immediately after his service, he found that getting silver for jewelry was difficult (it was a rationed commodity that traders worked hard to acquire), but "it was also difficult to sell it, too."

His late wife, Esther, did all the cutting of the turquoise, and he did the silverwork. "And then she goes out and sells it and gets all the money," he recalls, laughing. When it came to pricing, he and his wife set the price from the very beginning of their collaboration; there was no haggling when it came time to sell. It helped that when he started out he had no competition and that by the time he did, he was the acknowledged originator *and* master of Zuni needlepoint work.

He and Esther had eight children, all boys, and all helped their parents, learning from them in the process. But presently only two, Duwayne and Evan, make jewelry full-time. Bryant Jr. occasionally works silver, and son Robbie helps his father cut the stones that go into his work. Grandson Lance is now making jewelry, too.

By the early 1960s Bryant had given up gasoline torches and switched over to acetylene. With electricity available, he was also using power grinders and buffers. By then others were making needlepoint jewelry as well (some as early as the late 1940s).

There have been other changes in the decades since the 1960s. The boom period of the mid-1970s was one. "It used to be hard to sell during the winter, but not anymore, not since then." The boom period was intense for many smiths, and Bryant was no exception, being a high-profile artist. "People came by every day. Every day to buy. Sometimes the Arab traders would just come in, pick up the finished jewelry on my bench, and leave the money and go." It was during this time that he began to sign his work, at the request of the traders with whom he worked. When the Hunt Brothers famously ran the price of silver up from less than $5 an ounce to nearly $50, he quit buying the silver for his orders and had the traders provide the silver.

Like most jewelry artists of repute, he has seen his work copied by non-Indian, overseas sources, pieces that get sold without a tag indicating country of origin. "We all used to make our own designs and didn't have any problem at all," he says. "Now people are copying and trying to sell for less." But, like most Indian jewelers of his stature, it is the quality of his work that has been the best protection, as copyists sacrifice quality for price.

While he still makes his trademark needlepoint-row bracelets, he is continually designing new works, especially earrings. "I sketch out my own ideas. I draw it first, then work in silver." Showing a few small, actual-size sketches, he explains, "I do the drawings to help guide my work.

"I started out working at night but one of the buyers told me not to because it will ruin my eyes, but I did anyway." And so, like many if not most silversmiths, he still likes to work at night, when it is quiet and he can work late, and undisturbed, continuing quietly to create the work that has made him famous.

LORRAINE AND DUWAYNE WAATSA
ZUNI

LORRAINE QUAM WAATSA'S FAMILY is also famous for their jewelry. Her mother, Alice Ondelacy Quam, who works with *her* husband, Duane, has been famous for more than half a century for exceptional cluster work, which employs only the finest natural turquoise and coral. Alice and Duane learned the craft from *her* parents, Warren and Doris Ondelacy, who were well known for their cluster work as far back as 1930.

Recounts Lorraine, "I started making jewelry when I was eighteen. My teacher was my grandfather, and then my mom and dad. The first things I made were small cluster pendants. I still have the very first piece."

Though his family is known for its own needlepoint work, Duwayne (b. 1953) works with Lorraine (b. 1954) in cluster style, a technique he learned from her father roughly thirty-five years ago. When Duwayne and Lorraine collaborate, he does the silver and she the stonework, but they also work individually, with Duwayne tending to make larger bracelets and buckles, even concha belts, while Lorraine makes smaller pieces, including earrings and pendants. "We work with coral, turquoise, lapis, opal—whatever the buyer wants," says Lorraine. "I buy my own material. Sleeping Beauty turquoise is the easiest to work. Morenci and spiderweb turquoise can be brittle, but you never know until you start grinding. … I try to come up with new designs, and I'm trying to carry on what my parents worked. I do new designs in my head first, then I make the bezels for them and put them together on the silver base plate the way I see it in my head, and eventually it comes out to what I want."

LEE WEEBOTHEE
ZUNI

EVEN IN QUASI-RETIREMENT, Lee Weebothee ranks among the best and most talented of Zuni jewelers. His career, shared in large measure with his late wife, Mary (1934–95), spans nearly seventy years, with his training beginning in 1937, at age nine.

"My father was working silver then," he says. "When I got through chopping wood I would go inside and check on how he was doing. Sometimes he would be melting silver by the fireplace, and I would work the bellows." It was from his father that he learned how to hammer out sheet from ingot, the one aspect of the job he found hardest to learn and hardest to do.

Using the common methods of his time, Lee's father, Wilbur Weebothee, cast silver ingot to make his own sheet and wire. "He had a 'pull stone' outside with a drawplate on top," Lee remembers. "We used to use a Model T axle to pull the wire." From his father he also learned how to make his own silver solder, which he does to this day, rather than use store-bought solder.

"I got initiated [into a Zuni religious society], maybe when I was seven or eight," he says. "That is when I started watching how he worked. At that time he was working on squash blossoms. Three stones on each blossom. He cast a piece of silver six inches long. He then took that and heated it and bent it for the nazha. He stamped it with designs, first on the outside, then the inside. It took about a day and a half to make that necklace. That was the old style."

Lee's apprenticeship was typical for the time: one of watching and helping. One of the people he watched was the famed early Zuni silversmith Juan Dedios, who was his father's step-uncle. It was Juan who had taught Lee's father. In 1939, when he was a nine-year-old boy, Lee began watching his granduncle work. "I used to water the horses over there at a well next to his workshop. While they were drinking I'd go in and watch—quietly."

Lee's first opportunity to make a piece of jewelry from scratch came a few years later, at age twelve, when he pounded out a ring. "I got me some copper wire and practiced on that. We were over at Juan's, and I made a copper bracelet. He said, 'You make that? You should make some and take them in to Gallup and sell them for arthritis.'"

Watching Juan, Lee learned how to sand-cast. "I made crucifixes. I got smart then, and I used plaster of paris to make a mold. In Prohibition days that was my wine money," he laughs, adding, "[Later, when] Mary was making thunderbirds in stone and shell, we used to say that was her [basketball] game money."

His humor aside, the economics of jewelry-making have always loomed large, not only in the lives of individual smiths, but in the village itself, as goods from far and wide were traded for their work. "Dad sold mostly to the eastern Pueblos. They used to come here in the fall and sell baskets and strings of chile. Lots of folks from Jemez. [Mother] had about eight of them [plaited yucca baskets from Jemez] that she used for Shalako to hold bread and things."

At some point he started working for Robert Wallace. "He showed me some [single-row, five-stone] rings that he got from jewelry-maker Della Casi Appa. He wanted me to make some like these with the square stones. I made seven of them. He tried to pay me in cash, but I wanted something to eat. I took a slab of bacon instead. I was so proud."

After he and Mary were married, "We started on the cluster business. The designs were all Mary's ideas. Mary never drew out her designs; they were always in her head. I wasn't much of an artist"—he laughs—"but in the silver department …" Together they had nine children, all of whom learned jewelry-making from their parents, though many of them work at other jobs, from teaching to sales clerking.

They sold to several different traders. One complained about price: "We had an argument about price. He had been paying cheap prices from the Navajo. But our work was better. So I made a deal with him—either pay my price or deal with the Navajos," Lee says, laughing.

"One day Joe Tanner [a well-known Gallup trader] came by the house with some very nice turquoise. He said, 'Mary, I want you to pick out something and make something real good, and if I sell it we will go into business.'

"She said, 'They are not all the same color.'

"Joe replied, 'No, they are not all the same color … You can do better matching it up than I can.'

"'Oh all right,' she said. So we just started cluster. I made the bezel work and Mary did the cutting and polishing, and it turned out real nice. When I finished it Joe came over. He didn't even knock, he just came in and asked, 'Did you finish that thing?'

"'Yes' I said, 'but I think you better sit down.' He got excited. That made us feel good. We were always concerned about the reaction we would get when we made the jewelry."

Lee and Mary started entering pieces in the Gallup Intertribal Ceremonial in the 1970s, earning prize after prize, but then they stopped entering their work. "We were hogging all the prizes," says Lee. "We were talking about this but one year we decided not to enter, to let the younger generation get up on the ladder. They wanted us to keep on entering prize-winning stuff, but we were well-known already." It is a decision consciously made by virtually every top silversmith I have met: teach, encourage, and make room for the next generation of jewelry artists.

Patience is a virtue when learning any new skill and a crucial one when perfecting it. Lee says his father told him that "if you can't make something work, don't get mad at it. Get away from it for a while. And to this day if I am beginning to lose patience I take my father's advice."

Lee suffered a stroke a few years ago but has applied that same patience and diligence to his recovery. He may not create as much jewelry as he once did, but he still works at his craft, sometimes relying on one of his sons to help with the stampwork.

And his sense of humor still shines through as he recounts stories from earlier days: "We went down there (Phoenix) for about six shows—at the Heard Museum and the Scottsdale National. Then we went to San Diego, where our work won three awards. I was speaking on TV that night, because Mary did not want to talk. I guess I did a pretty good job, because the next day crowds came in to see us. Some asked where I went to school because I spoke so well. I told them, 'I went to Zuni College. After fifteen years they gave us white pieces of paper and told us to go home and not come back: You're educated Indians now.'"

Lee is well-known for a particular texture he creates for many of his rings. People have copied it, but they don't create it his way, and as a result their copies don't match up with the original. Asked how he creates the effect, Lee smiles. "It's a secret. Even my kids don't know."

ALTON AND KEE YAZZIE
NAVAJO

THERE WAS A TIME WHEN MANY PEOPLE IN TRIBES across the country spoke two or more languages. At Hano Village, on the Hopi Reservation, some children are raised speaking Hopi, Tewa, and English; in the past, a few also learned to speak Navajo, Zuni, or Spanish. Navajo jewelry artist Kee Yazzie speaks several languages, but for him those languages include a few more far-flung: Laotian, Thai, and Cambodian, learned while studying for missionary work with the LDS church in Boston.

Born in 1969, he went to school in Ganado, Arizona, and attended community college in Utah, where he studied architecture. In 1993, shortly after returning to Arizona and settling in Winslow, he says, "Ray Scott came by my house and asked if I wanted to learn." Scott, a silversmith for nearly twenty years at that point, needed a couple of apprentices to meet the demand for his work. So Kee, along with Chris Billy, began learning the basics, beginning with polishing. He quickly graduated to soldering, forming, and design work. Scott mentored his apprentices well, introducing them to the Indian art show circuit and teaching them the skills necessary to market one's work. By 1995 Kee had acquired all his own tools and soon was able to strike out on his own.

Kee had learned from Scott that it is not so much the skills that you have but the way you apply them. "There are so many jewelers doing amazing work," he says, citing Mike Bird Romero, Norbert Beshligaii, and the husband-wife team of Gail Bird and Yazzie Johnson, "that I knew I had to create something different. I grew up around a lot of rock

ABOVE: *Alton Yazzie.*
OPPOSITE PAGE: *Kee Yazzie.*

art, so some of that has influenced my work." But he has found many other sources of design inspiration, some of which inspired his "underwater bracelet" of sea motifs.

Stampwork and overlay work (up to four layers) are his primary silverwork techniques, employed in a wide range of ways to execute his constantly evolving designs. In 1997 he began to work in gold as well, primarily as an accent. Turquoise was the first stone he used, later adding coral.

"I started off selling direct to galleries, with Blue Rain being my first gallery client," he says. "A couple years later, in 1998, I showed at Indian Market and earned a first-prize ribbon for a bracelet. The following year I began showing at the Heard show."

A silversmith's tools are his livelihood—and sometimes more. "My most valuable tools are my stamps. My dad made my stamps." His father, Alton, learned jewelry-making from his father and from his father's father, John Bedonie, grandfather to several prominent Navajo silversmiths. Alton left full-time jewelry-making in 1971 to take a job with the Winslow City Water Department. Now a supervisor, Alton says, "I'm looking forward to retiring and having more time to work silver." His current style uses overlay and engraving techniques.

Work by Kee Yazzie.

One of six children, Kee is the only one to forge a career as a jewelry artist, but he and his wife, Tammy (a teacher), have two young boys, so there may be a fourth generation of silversmiths in the Yazzie family.

Alton and Kee Yazzie.

STEVE YELLOWHORSE
NAVAJO

STEVE YELLOWHORSE IS A THIRD-GENERATION member of the Yellowhorse family of entrepreneurs, descended from Arthur Beasley (Ponca Indian on his mother's side), who built the Navajo Castle on the old Route 66 near Lupton, Arizona, and Anna Tahe Yellowhorse, daughter of Cut Hair Yellowhorse and granddaughter of Hosteen Belihnłsoh (Mister Yellowhorse). Steve's father was the redoubtable Juan Yellowhorse (born William D. Beasley), an entrepreneur extraordinaire who came to be called Chief Yellowhorse. His mother was Constance Goddu, from Boston. In Steve's generation there are more than fifty cousins (his dad was the oldest of nine children), many of whom either make or sell jewelry. Others have branched out into a wide range of occupations and businesses, with the fourth generation showing no sign that the remarkable entrepreneurial legacy of the Yellowhorse Clan is in any way diminishing.

Born in 1954, in Corpus Christi, Texas, while his dad was in the Navy, Steve wound up going to school in Sanders, Arizona, a ways east of the Painted Desert. A bright student, after his junior year he was selected for Dartmouth's ABC program for summer school and spent his senior year in high school in Carmel, California. "I was a bit of a paradox: an angry, failing, straight-A student," he says. "While I was at Carmel I took classes in biology, history, and humanities from Ralf Kahl—one of those teachers that all the students loved because he was real. He had a tremendous positive influence on me. I lived with him and his family for a couple years after I got out of high school, then moved to back to Gallup."

In early 1975, at age twenty, Steve started working silver. "I kind of fell into it," he says. "I started with cement-and-oil casting. Tried that for a year but couldn't make a living at it, couldn't get it to cast right. Almost starved."

He then worked in several Gallup production shops, "learning the basics as I went along," working with and learning from fellow silversmiths Kevin Barnhill and Tom Taylor. He tried a few shows, including the Flagstaff Powwow (now defunct), where he found a tool so handy and indispensable that he uses it to this day: a revolving soldering tray. He bought it for $40—his net sales for the day.

In 1979 he married Antoinette Shorty, and together they began a family that now includes Mark, Sandra, and Amy. By the late 1970s he was self-employed again, working silver successfully on his own. His desire and willingness to experiment, coupled with some helpful suggestions from Gallup store owner Chet Jones and jewelry wholesaler Leon Ingram, led him to the creation of his own distinctive style of silverwork. He describes his inspiration sources as "natural design," Art Nouveau, modern art, and music, specifically jazz and virtuoso guitar.

Unlike many fellow silversmiths of the era, rather than travel extensively, selling retail at shows, Steve started out wholesaling, preferring to stay in Gallup with his family. In the mid-1980s he began to use gold in some of his work, and about the same time (1985) he began to work with Turney's shop in Gallup, a successful collaboration that lasted for fifteen years—until the death of Steve's father in 1999.

His father's death was a turning point. Since then, with his own children grown or nearly grown, Steve has begun to travel the West and Midwest, doing museum shows and retail shows and broadening his search for galleries to represent his work. As a part of that process, he produced a documentary film to explain his family history and the creative processes involved in his work.

Working now in a shop that is part of the sprawling state-line Yellowhorse family complex of shops and businesses (and close to where his brother Stuart and nephew Alvin also work silver), Steve finds that the market has changed since he began more than a quarter of a century ago: "A lot of the market is the lowest common denominator, a trinket mentality that stifles creativity, but there is still a market for quality, uniqueness, and that is who I am making jewelry for," he declares. To that end he constantly pushes himself to create new designs, leaving previous styles behind once he feels he has fully explored them.

Of his three children, only Mark makes jewelry—for piercings. Mark is also a musician, playing the guitar, bass, and drums. All of Steve's children play instruments. And what does Steve play? Recordings of guitar music as he cuts and solders, and jazz when he buffs and polishes. The music flows into his work as he observes, "One of the things I have to continually address is the preconceived idea many people have about how an American Indian should 'look.' My father is Navajo and my mother is French-Irish, and I'm an enrolled member of the Navajo tribe. When I do a show, one of my purposes is to educate people and shatter the misconception that all American Indians are alike. The truth is that we exist in as many colors, shapes, sizes, persuasions, and religious beliefs as can be imagined."

ACKNOWLEDGMENTS

No book is written solely by the author. It is always the result of collaboration and help. The artists deserve both acknowledgement and my deep thanks for agreeing to share their stories. There would be no book without them. The text was enormously enhanced by the work of photographers Robert Morrison, David Burckhalter, Bill Faust, Bruce Hucko, Ross Humphreys, and my youngest son, Santiago Bahti.

Others who loaned items to be photographed, provided contact information, advice or quotes include (in no special order) Martha Streuver, Roger Thomas, John Kennedy Sr., Tobe Turpen Jr., Tony Reyna, Bob and Maryann Kapoun, Fannie Etsitty, Joseph and Janice Day, Bill Faust, and Wayne Bobrick, as well as Navajo businessman Ron Benally and Joe Douthitt of Towayalane Trading, who was one of the first to lend a hand on this project and who was there at the very end of the project, scaring up jewelry for the very last photo. Thank you all.

GLOSSARY

anticlastic raising: a metalwork technique that involves hammering and shaping a single piece of metal into two opposing curved surfaces

bead-blasting: similar to sandblasting

bezel: a thin strip of silver soldered to a base plate, encircling the edge of a stone and holding it firm

bola: also known as a **bolo** tie, this is a type of necktie consisting of a piece of cord with an ornamental clasp that slides up and down to adjust for fit

bowguard (also *ketoh* or *gato*): a guard, originally of leather, worn to protect a man's wrist from the snap of a bow string

cabochon: a polished stone, usually slightly domed

channel work: a style of silverwork similar to mosaic except that each stone is set individually, separated by silver channels

chip inlay: utilizes an overlay technique with the recessed areas set with crushed stone, usually turquoise or coral and sometimes jet

cluster jewelry, cluster work: usually associated with Zuni jewelry style, but also made by Navajo jewelry artists; uses small stones grouped or "clustered" together, often in circular or oval patterns

concha: from the Spanish word for "shell," a round or oval piece of flat silver, usually with scalloped edges, used most often in a series on a belt; also sometimes called **concho**

coral: *Corallium rubrum*, a calcium carbonate with carotene created by colonies of the marine coral polyp; used to be imported primarily from the Mediterranean, but now most comes from the Sea of Japan

doming: forming a rounded or convex surface on silver

drawplate: a hard steel plate with a hole or series of holes through which wires are drawn to be made thinner and longer

engraving: scratching lines into a metal surface

flux: a substance that aids in soldering by cleaning the pieces of metal to be joined

hallmark: a mark on jewelry used to indicate the artist who made the piece; when used by a store or workshop it is called a "shopmark"

heishe: from the word used at Santo Domingo Pueblo for "shell"—traditionally refers to necklaces of flat, disk-shaped beads of shell or stone; also spelled **heishi**

hollowware: formed metal vessels such as bowls, pitchers, and teapots

ingot: a mass of metal, cast in a form (such as a bar or block) for easy handling and storage before it is worked to make jewelry and other objects; ingots may be rolled or hammered into sheets

jocla (also spelled **zhocla**): from the Navajo word for earring, a loop of mostly turquoise beads, traditionally worn as an earring, but which may be hung from a necklace and has evolved into a necklace ornament as well

lost-wax casting: a technique in which a wax model is used to create a mold from which the wax is then melted away and molten metal poured in to create the final piece; this technique can be used for one-of-a-kind works as well as production copies

nazha (sometimes spelled **naja**): a crescent-shaped pendant, popularly thought to be of Moorish inspiration, that often hangs from squash-blossom necklaces (from the Navajo word for crescent)

needlepoint: a form of cluster work in which the stones are very narrow and elongated in shape

overlay: a design cut from one piece of silver (or gold), soldered onto a plain piece of silver, and then oxidized

petit-point: a form of cluster jewelry using very tiny round or teardrop-shaped pieces of stone

planishing: smoothing metal by hammering

repoussé: a raised design formed on one side of metal by hammering from the underside

sand-cast: pouring molten silver or gold into a mold, usually made of oil and sand or tuff

soldering: the fusing of two pieces of metal using a heat that melts a lower-temperature metal that joins the two

spondylus shell (also called spiny oyster shell): a prized reddish-orange-to-red oyster shell from the Pacific coast of Baja California and the northwest coast of South America

squash-blossom: a necklace style usually employing silver beads with a series of pendant forms with petals, identified as "squash blossoms" (actually inspired by the form of a pomegranate), usually including a naja pendant

stampwork: using decorative metal stamps to impress designs into the surface of the silver

tab necklace: a stone or shell bead necklace alternating with larger flat tabs of stone or shell

tufa-cast: see "sand-cast"

tuff: a volcanic rock carved out for sand-cast work, often mistakenly called "tufa"

turquoise: a semiprecious stone found in arid regions such as the American Southwest, China, Chile and Iran; a hydrous aluminum phosphate colored by copper salts, and ranging in color from pale green to deep blue

INDIAN MARKETS AND FAIRS

Here is a rough overview of the major annual events around the country where you might be able to see some of these artists' work. The dates may vary from year to year, and the size of these shows and number of vendors are also widely variable. Most important, some are juried and some are not, so you may see differing degrees of expertise among the presenting artists.

January, **Colorado Indian Market,** Denver, CO

January or February, **Native American Arts Festival,** Litchfield Park, AZ

February, **Southwest Indian Art Fair,** Arizona State Museum, Tucson, AZ

February, **Tulsa Indian Arts Festival,** Tulsa, OK

February, **O'odham Tash Fair and All-Indian Rodeo,** Casa Grande, AZ

March, **Heard Museum Guild Indian Fair and Market,** Phoenix, AZ

April, **Gathering of Nations,** Albuquerque, NM

April, **Indian Arts and Crafts Association Show,** Albuquerque, NM

May or June, **Red Earth Festival,** Oklahoma City, OK

June, **Eiteljorg Museum Indian Market,** Indianapolis, IN

June, **Museum of Man Indian Market,** San Diego, CA

July, **Eight Northern Indian Pueblos Arts and Crafts Show,** San Juan Pueblo, NM

July, **Southern California Indian Center Powwow,** Los Angeles, CA

July (sometimes also late June), **Hopi Festival of Arts and Culture,** Museum of Northern Arizona, Flagstaff, AZ

July, **Prescott Indian Art Market,** Sharlot Hall Museum, Prescott, AZ

July, **Zuni Cultural Arts Expo,** Zuni Pueblo, NM

August, **Inter-Tribal Indian Ceremonial,** Gallup, NM

August, **Navajo Festival of Arts and Culture,** Museum of Northern Arizona, Flagstaff, AZ

August, **Santa Fe Indian Market,** Santa Fe, NM

September, **Navajo Nation Fair,** Window Rock, AZ

September–October, **Lawrence Indian Arts Show,** Lawrence, KS

Columbus Day weekend, **Tuhisma Hopi Indian Arts and Crafts Market,** Kykotsmovi, AZ

October, **Northern Navajo Nation Fair,** Shiprock, AZ

November, **Southwest Museum Indian Market,** Los Angeles, CA

December, **Pueblo Grande Museum Indian Market,** Phoenix, AZ

Rio Nuevo Publishers®

P.O. Box 5250, Tucson, Arizona 85703-0250

(520) 623-9558, www.rionuevo.com

Text copyright © 2007 by Mark Bahti. Photographs copyright © 2007 by W. Ross Humphreys, except as follows: Mark Bahti pages 32 (top), 58, 61, 66 (bottom), 91, 118 (top), 128, 142 (bottom), 146 (bottom); Santiago Bahti page 136; Wayne Bobrick pages 27, 28, 29; David Burckhalter page 111 (right); Bill Faust page 51 (bottom); Bruce Hucko page 26.; Bob Morrison pages 20, 54 (top), 133, 166 (top, bottom), 167, 177 (top), 206 (top); courtesy of Maria Samora pages 144-147 (except for page 146 bottom).

Jewelry shown on pages 2–5 is by the following artists: p. 2 Dorothy Poleyma, p. 4 left Bryant Waatsa Sr., p. 4 right Steve LaRance, p. 5 left Joseph and Mary Calabaza, p. 5 right Cheyenne Harris.

All rights reserved. No part of this book may be reproduced, stored, introduced into a retrieval system, or otherwise copied in any form without the prior written permission of the publisher, except for brief quotations in reviews or citations.

Library of Congress Cataloging-in-Publication Data

Bahti, Mark.

Silver and stone : profiles of American Indian jewelers / Mark Bahti.

   p. cm.

ISBN 978-1-887896-35-1

ISBN 978-1-933855-29-5 (pbk.)

1. Indians of North America—Southwest, New—Jewelry. 2. Indian silverwork—Southwest, New. 3. Indian jewelers—Southwest, New—Biography. I. Title.

E78.S7B172 2007

739.27092'397079—dc22

                        2007025548

Design: Karen Schober, Seattle, Washington.

Printed in Korea.

10 9 8 7 6 5 4 3 2 1